3

4

Volume 8: How to Apply Response Surface Methodology

Revised Edition

The ASQC Basic References in Quality Control: Statistical Techniques
Samuel S. Shapiro, Ph.D, and Edward F. Mykytka, Ph.D., Editors

Volume 8: How to Apply Response Surface Methodology

by John A. Cornell

**How to Apply Response
Surface Methodology**

by John A. Cornell

Library of Congress Cataloging-in-Publication Data

Cornell, John A.
  How to apply response surface methodology / by
John A. Cornell.—2nd ed.
  p. cm.—(The ASQC basic references in quality control :
statistical techniques ; v. 8)
  Includes bibliographical references. (p.   ).
  1. Response surfaces (Statistics) I. Title. II. Series: ASQC
basic references in quality control ; v. 8.
QA279.C663 1990
519.5—dc20   90–34649
                                                      CIP

10987654321
ISBN 0–87389–092–2

Acquisitions Editor: Jeanine L. Lau
Production Editor: Tammy Griffin
Set in Times by A-R Editions, Inc. Cover design by Artistic License.
Printed and bound by BookCrafters.

Printed in the United States of America

ASQC
310 WEST WISCONSIN AVENUE
MILWAUKEE, WISCONSIN 53203
414/272-8575 FAX: 414/272-1734

The Basic References in Quality Control: Statistical Techniques (Samuel S. Shapiro, PhD, and Edward F. Mykytka, PhD, co-editors) is a continuing literature project of ASQC's Statistics Division. Its aim is to present the latest statistical techniques in a form which is easily followed by the quality control practitioner so that these procedures can be readily applied to solve industrial quality problems.

Suggestions as to subject matters to be covered and format of the booklets are welcome and will be considered in future editions. Such suggestions should be sent to one of the co-editors.

Volumes Published
Volume 1: How to Analyze Data with Simple Plots (W. Nelson)
Volume 2: How to Perform Continuous Sampling (CSP) (K. S. Stephens)
**Volume 3: How to Test Normality and Other Distributional Assumptions,
   Revised Edition** (S. S. Shapiro)
Volume 4: How to Perform Skip-Lot and Chain Sampling (K. S. Stephens)
**Volume 5: How to Run Mixture Experiments for Product Quality,
   Revised Edition** (J. A. Cornell)
Volume 6: How to Analyze Reliability Data (W. Nelson)
**Volume 7: How and When to Perform Bayesian Acceptance Sampling
   (Plus a Blast with TNT), Revised Edition** (T. W. Calvin)
Volume 8: How to Apply Response Surface Methodology, Revised Edition (J. A. Cornell)
**Volume 9: How to Use Regression Analysis in Quality Control,
   Revised Edition** (D. C. Crocker)
Volume 10: How to Plan an Accelerated Life Test—Some Practical Guidelines
   (W. Q. Meeker and G. J. Hahn)
Volume 11: How to Perform Statistical Tolerance Analysis (N. D. Cox)
Volume 12: How to Choose the Proper Sample Size (G. G. Brush)
Volume 13: How to Use Sequential Statistical Methods (T. P. Williams)

The ASQC Basic References in Quality Control: Statistical Techniques is a literature project of the Statistics Division of the ASQC. The series' review board consists of Saul Blumenthal, Joseph W. Foster, Alan J. Gross, Gerald J. Hahn, Norman L. Johnson, H. Alan Lasater, Edward A. Sylvestre and Harrison M. Wadsworth Jr., supplemented (for the current volume, eighth in the series) by J. Stuart Hunter.

In the Statistics Division Newsletter, Volume 1, Number 1 (February 21, 1980), Philip B. Crosby (President, ASQC) called the comprehension and handling of statistics ". . . the most basic of needs for all of us . . . ." He went on to state that, "Without numerical information in its most precise form, we cannot complete our responsibility to management and other fellow employees. And without the tools to first comprehend and then explain the analysis, we are equally impotent."

This booklet describes in a clear, *how to* format the fundamental techniques of *response surface methodology* (RSM). RSM is a set of techniques designed to find the best value of a response and to map the contours of the response surface — in order to gain a better understanding of the overall response system. It makes use of the statistical techniques included in the objects regression and design of experiments. The booklet describes a number of the most used experimental designs and the subsequent analyses used with the RSM technology. An annotated bibliography is included to guide the reader to more advanced phases of the subject.

The author, Dr. John A. Cornell, is a professor at the University of Florida in Gainesville, FL. He is an applied statistician who has had extensive practical experience in the subject and he is the coauthor, with André I. Khuri, of the text *Response Surfaces: Designs and Analyses*. This booklet arises from his experiences and hence he is able to highlight the important aspects of the subject from the viewpoint of the quality engineer.

Samuel S. Shapiro
Florida International University
Miami, Florida
June 1984

Abstract

Response surface methodology consists of a set of techniques used in the empirical study of relationships between one or more responses and a group of input variables. This booklet explains how to exploit simple empirical models such as first- and second-degree polynomials to approximate a relationship between a response variable and the input variables over a selected region of interest. Also covered are designs for collecting response values for fitting the polynomials as well as how to determine how well the model fits. A sequential approach to locating the region of highest response values (where highest is considered best) is presented and is illustrated with data from an industrial experiment. A comprehensive set of references is given to allow for further study of the techniques and principles.

1

1.0 Introduction

Many experimental programs are designed with a two-fold purpose in mind: to quantify the relationship between the values of some measurable response variable(s) and those of a set of experimental factors presumed to affect the response(s) and, to find the values of the factors that produce the best value or values of the response(s). For example, upon ascertaining that the purity of an end product of a chemical process is affected by the concentrations of several reagents in the solution as well as the temperature of the reaction, the chemist would then try to determine the specific concentrations of the reagents and the temperature level that results in the highest degree of purity of the product. As another example, suppose a series of clinical trials is conducted on patients with high blood pressure where the patients are given selected combinations of two drugs each known to reduce their blood pressure reading. Here again the purpose of administering several combinations of the drugs to the various individuals is to find the specific combination of drugs that reduces the patients' blood pressure reading by the greatest amount during some specified interval of time.

Response surface methodology (RSM) is a set of techniques designed to find the "best" value of the response. If discovering the best value or values of the response is beyond the available resources of the experiment, then response surface methods are used to at least gain *a better understanding of the overall response system*. These techniques, first introduced by Box and Wilson (1951) and later developed by Box and Hunter (1957) and others such as Bradley (1958), Davies (1960), and Hunter (1958, 1959a, 1959b), consist of designing the experiment and the subsequent analysis of the experimental data. In most cases, the behavior of the measured response is governed by certain laws which can be approximated by a deterministic relationship between the response and the set of experimental factors, and thus it should be possible to determine the best conditions (levels) of the factors to optimize a desired output. Usually this relationship is either too complex or unknown and an empirical approach is necessary. The strategy employed in such an approach is the basis of *response surface methods,* hereafter abbreviated RSM.

1.1 The Similarity of Regression Analysis and Response Surface Methodology

In any system in which variable quantities change and the interest is to assess the effects of several factors on the behavior of some measurable quantity (the response), such an assessment is possible through a *regression analysis*. In regression, data are collected from an experiment. The data are then used to empirically quantify, through some form of mathematical model, the relationship that exists between the response variable and its influencing factors. The response variable is called the *dependent* variable or the *response* and the influencing factors are referred to as *explanatory* or *regressor* variables. Regression analysis is one of the most widely used tools for investigative purposes having applications in many fields including the physical, biological, and social sciences, as well as engineering.

Response surface methods are techniques employed before, during, and after a regression analysis is performed on the data. Preceding the analysis the experiment must be designed; that is, the explanatory variables must be selected and the values to be used during the actual experimentation must be designated. After the regression analysis, certain optimization techniques are applied. Thus, the subject of RSM includes application of regression and other techniques in an attempt to gain a better understanding of the characteristics of the response system under study.

Some of the basic terminology that will be used throughout this booklet will be reviewed as an appropriate introduction to the subject of regression and the topic of RSM. For simplicity of presentation it will be assumed that there is only one response variable to be studied, although in practice there are usually several response variables that are under investigation simultaneously.

1.1.1 Terminology: Factors

Factors are processing conditions that are presumed to influence the values of the response variable. In the chemical purity example mentioned previously, the factors were the processing temperature and the specific chemical reagents in the process. If the rate of the chemical reaction is also known to affect the purity and the rate (or length of time of the reaction) can be controlled, then reaction rate would also be a factor to consider. As another example, in an agricultural soybean experiment where the yield is known to be affected by the amounts of nitrogen (N), phosphorous (P), and potassium (K) making up the fertilizer blend, the three factors are N, P, and K. A possible fourth factor could be the frequency of application of the fertilizer to the plots.

Factors in a regression analysis can be qualitative, such as the type of fertilizer, or the sex of an applicant seeking a position, or catalyst type, or the vendor supplying the material. On the other hand, factors can be quantitative, such as the level of temperature or the amount of fertilizer applied. In most response surface investigations, if the qualitative factors can be considered as blocking variables (see Section 4.3), then the specific factors to be studied in detail are those that are quantitative in nature and their levels are assumed to be fixed or controlled (without error) by the experimenter. Factors and their levels will be denoted by ξ_1, ξ_2, . . . , ξ_k and X_1, X_2, . . . , X_k, respectively.

The response is the measurable quantity whose value is assumed to be affected by changing the levels of the factors and whose values we are most interested in optimizing. In the chemical purity example, the response was the *purity* of the end product, whereas in the agricultural experiment the response was the *yield* of soybeans measured in pounds harvested per plot. The true value of the response corresponding to any particular combination of the factor levels is denoted by η. The objective of the experiment is to try to maximize or minimize η or at the very best, to determine the region of best values of η. The term, "true response, η," is meant the hypothetical value of η that would be obtained in the absence of experimental error of any kind. (Note that experimental error is defined as variability in the observed values of a product formed from the same set of experimental conditions, and this variability can be caused by factors that have not been included in the experiment.) However, because experimental error is present in all experiments, the response value that is actually observed for any particular combination of factor levels differs from η and is denoted by Y, that is, $Y = \eta + \epsilon$, where ϵ represents experimental error.

1.1.2 Response

When we say that the true value of the response η depends upon the levels X_1, $X_2, \ldots, X_k$ of k quantitative factors, $\xi_1, \xi_2, \ldots, \xi_k$, we are saying that there exists some mathematical function of $X_1, X_2, \ldots, X_k$, the value of which for any given combination of factor levels supplies the corresponding value of η, that is,

1.1.3 The Response Function

$$\eta = \phi(X_1, X_2, \ldots, X_k).$$

The function ϕ is called the true response function and ϕ is assumed to be a continuous function of the X_i.

To represent the relationship $\eta = \phi(X_1)$ between η and the levels of the single factor ξ_1, a mathematical equation or model called a *polynomial model* may be used. If the functional relationship ϕ is smooth, it is possible to represent it locally to any required degree of approximation with a Taylor Series expansion about some point ξ_{10}; thus,

1.1.4 The Polynomial Representation of a Response Surface

$$\eta = \phi(\xi_{10}) + (\xi_1 - \xi_{10})\phi'(\xi_{10}) + \tfrac{1}{2}[\xi_1 - \xi_{10}]^2\phi''(\xi_{10}) + \cdots \tag{1}$$

The expansion (1) reduces to a polynomial of the form

$$\eta = \phi(X_1) = \beta_0 + \beta_1 X_1 + \beta_{11} X_1^2 + \cdots \tag{2}$$

where the coefficients β_0, β_1, and β_{11} are multiples of the partial derivatives of $\phi(\xi_1)$ and X_1 is the value of ξ_1. The successive terms, β_0, $\beta_1 X_1$, and $\beta_{11} X_1^2$, of the polynomial are said to be of degree 0, 1, 2, and so on. By taking terms up to degree 1 only the model expression yields the equation of a straight line, i.e., $\eta = \beta_0 + \beta_1 X_1$. By taking terms up to degree 2, the model becomes an equation for a parabola

$$\eta = \beta_0 + \beta_1 X_1 + \beta_{11} X_1^2$$

which is shown in Figure 1a.

For two factors ξ_1 and ξ_2, the polynomial equation is

$$\eta = \phi(X_1, X_2) = \beta_0 + \beta_1 X_1 + \beta_2 X_2 + \beta_{11} X_1^2 + \beta_{22} X_2^2 + \beta_{12} X_1 X_2 + \cdots \quad (3)$$

An example of a second-order model is given by the gelatin cohesiveness surface model shown in Figure 1b. This is a second-degree polynomial in X_1 and X_2 and contains six terms.

The constants β_0, β_1, . . . , β_{12} in Eq. (3) are called *regression coefficients*. The variables X_1 and X_2 are called *explanatory variables* in the regression function. If the polynomial equation (3) exactly represents the response function $\phi(X_1, X_2)$ in the region of ξ_1 and ξ_2 under study, then β_0 is the level of the response at $X_1 = 0$ and $X_2 = 0$ and β_0 is only meaningful if the values of $X_1 = 0$ and $X_2 = 0$ appear within the experimental region. As mentioned previously, the coefficients β_1 and β_2 are the values of the first order differential coefficients $\partial\phi/\partial X_1$ and $\partial\phi/\partial X_2$ at $X_1 = X_2 = 0$ and may be referred to as the *first-order effects. The coefficients* β_{11}, β_{22}, and β_{12} are defined as $\frac{1}{2}\partial^2\phi/\partial X_1^2$, $\frac{1}{2}\partial^2\phi/\partial X_2^2$ and $\partial^2\phi/\partial X_1\partial X_2$, respectively, and are referred to as *second-order effects,* and so on.

1.1.5 The Predicted Response Function

The structural form of ϕ is usually unknown and thus an approximating form of ϕ is sought using a polynomial (2) or (3) or some other empirical form of model equation. The approximation is accomplished by first choosing some number of experiments to be performed at various combinations of the levels $X_1, X_2, \ldots, X_k$ of the k factors. At each factor level combination, an observed value of the response is recorded and the observations are then used to arrive at the form of the approximating equation or predicted response function. Generally, the success of a response surface investigation depends on whether the degree of the approximating polynomial can be fixed at 1 or 2 since low-degree models contain fewer terms than higher-degree models and thus require fewer experiments to be performed.

To illustrate, assume that the true response function written in terms of the levels of the two factors ξ_1 and ξ_2 can be expressed locally using the equation of a plane which is the first-degree polynomial

$$\eta = \beta_0 + \beta_1 X_1 + \beta_2 X_2 \quad (4)$$

where β_0, β_1, and β_2 are unknown parameters or regression coefficients to be estimated and X_1 and X_2 represent the experimental levels of ξ_1 and ξ_2, respec-

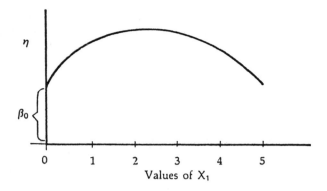

Figure 1a
The curve $\eta = \beta_0 + \beta_1 X_1 + \beta_{11} X_1^2$, where $\beta_1 > 0$ and $\beta_{11} < 0$

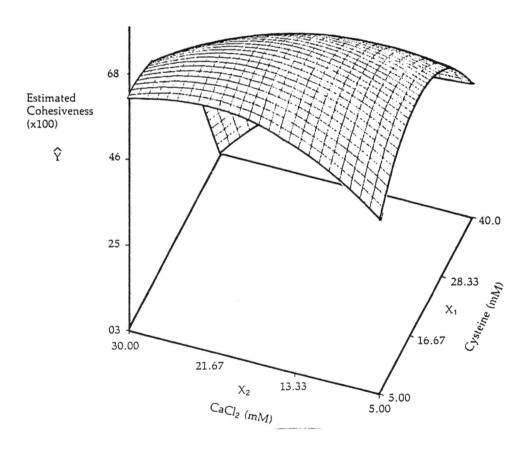

Figure 1b
Estimated cohesiveness surface of whey protein gelatin generated by the equation $\hat{Y} = 22.53 + 2.56X_1 + 3.07X_2 - 0.057X_1^2 - 0.062X_2^2 - 0.056X_1X_2$

tively. Having collected some number $N \geq 3$ of observed response values (Y), the estimates b_0, b_1, and b_2 of the parameters β_0, β_1, and β_2, respectively, are obtained using the method of least squares (Section 2). After it is decided that the parameter estimates b_0, b_1, and b_2 are useful in relaying information about the value of the response, then the unknown parameters in Equation 4 are replaced by their respective estimates to produce the prediction equation

$$\hat{Y} = b_0 + b_1X_1 + b_2X_2 \tag{5}$$

where $\hat{Y}$, (read ''Y hat''), denotes the predicted or estimated value of η for given values of X_1 and X_2. Of course, before any predictions are made with (5), it must be determined that the predictions at the data collection points in the experimental region are close to the observed data values. In Section 2.5 ways of testing the adequacy of empirical models fitted to the data will be discussed.

1.1.6 The Response Surface

The relationship $\eta = \phi(X_1)$ between η and the levels of the single factor ξ_1 may be represented by a straight line or by a curve as shown in Figure 1a. The relationship $\eta = \phi(X_1, X_2, \ldots, X_k)$ between η and the levels of k factors $\xi_1, \xi_2, \ldots, \xi_k$ may be represented by a *surface*. For $k = 2$, an estimated second-order whey protein gelatin surface is shown in Figure 1b where $\hat{Y}$ represents the estimated cohesiveness (x 100) of the gelatin, X_1 is the level of cysteine, and X_2 is the level of calcium chloride ($CaCl_2$) used in the formation of the gelatin. The observed values of cohesiveness were each multiplied by 100 to eliminate the number of decimal places for the response contours as well as to reduce the number of decimal places for the estimated coefficients in the second-order response equation that produced the surface in Figure 1b,

$$\hat{Y} = 22.53 + 2.56X_1 + 3.07X_2 - 0.057X_1^2 - 0.062X_2^2 - 0.056X_1X_2. \tag{6}$$

With k factors, the response surface is of dimensionality $k + 1$, so that the curve in Figure 1a is depicted in 2 dimensions, whereas the surface in Figure 1b is visualized in 3 dimensions; the 3rd dimension being the height of the surface above the 2-dimensional plane of the values of X_1 and X_2.

1.1.7 Contour Representation of a Response Surface

A technique used to help us in visualizing the shape of a three-dimensional response surface is the plotting of contours of the response surface. In a contour plot, lines or curves of equal response values are drawn on a graph or plane whose coordinates represent the levels of the factors. The lines (or curves) are known as *contours* of the surface. Each contour represents a specific value for the height of the surface (that is, a specific value of $\hat{Y}$), above the plane defined for combinations of the levels of the factors. The plotting of different surface height values enables one to focus attention on the levels of the factors at which the changes in the surface height occur. A contour plot of the estimated gelatin cohesiveness (x 100) surface in Figure 1b is illustrated in Figure 2, where only the estimated cohesiveness values inside the boundary of the experimental region are valid.

Contour plotting is not limited to depicting surfaces in one and two dimensions. A familiarity with the geometrical representation for two and three factors enables the general situation for $k > 3$ factors to be more readily understood, although they cannot be visualized geometrically. For example, if in addition to the levels of $CaCl_2$ (X_2), and of cysteine (X_1), a third factor, the temperature of reaction X_3, is included, then contour surfaces of equal cohesiveness could be drawn in the plane of X_1 and X_2 for several values of X_3.

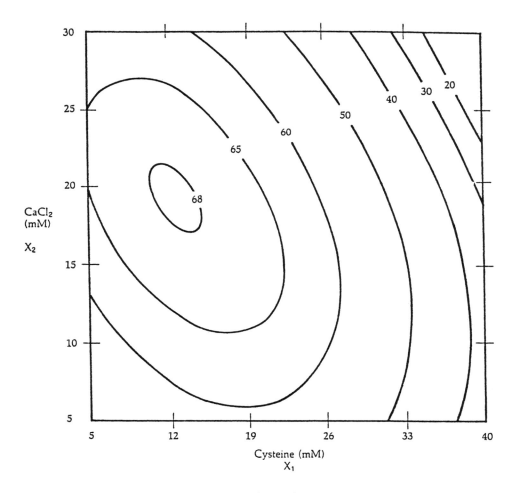

Figure 2
Contour plot of the gelatin cohesiveness surface (contour values are cohesiveness times 100.)

1.1.8 The Experimental Region

At the preliminary stages of a response surface investigation the experimenter is usually asked to specify the region of conceivable factor level values that represents the factor combinations of potential interest. This can be done by specifying the value of each of the factors that represents the current operating conditions and if a neighborhood about the current conditions is to be explored, then varying the amount of each factor by increasing and decreasing its value produces the experimental region. For example, former whey protein gelatins had been made using the approximate levels of cysteine and $CaCl_2$ of 21 mM and 16 mM, respectively. To investigate the effects of cysteine and $CaCl_2$ on the cohesiveness of the whey protein gelatin, the levels of each factor were to be varied so that the range of interest of cysteine was 5 mM to 40 mM while the range of interest of $CaCl_2$ was 5 mM to 30 mM. The *experimental region* of interest is therefore the rectangular region containing all combinations of values of X_1 and X_2 belonging to the intervals $5 \leq X_1 \leq 40$ mM and $5 \leq X_2 \leq 30$ mM. [Later in Section 2 we shall define the region of experimentation to be a circle.] During the experimentation only those values of X_1 and X_2 that fall within these ranges are used unless it is discovered during the initial set of experiments that it is necessary to explore levels of X_1 and X_2 that extend beyond the boundaries of the original region.

1.2 Questions to Consider When Planning a Response Surface Investigation

Simply stated, the questions to be answered in planning a response surface investigation are:

i. In setting up the experimental program, consideration must be given to:
   a. What response variables are to be measured, how they will be measured, and in what sequence?
   b. Which factors are most important and therefore will be included in the experiment, and which are least important and can these factors be omitted? With the important factors, can the desired effects be detected?
   c. What extraneous or disturbing factors must be controlled or at least have their effects minimized?
   d. What is the experimental unit, that is to say, what is the piece of experimental material from which a response value is measured? How are the experimental units to be replicated, if at all?

The choice of the factors and their levels determine the type and size of the experimental region. The number of levels of each factor as well as the number of replicated experimental units represent the total number of experiments that will be performed.

ii. Prior to deciding on the specific levels of each of the factors to be used, the following questions must be considered concerning the modeling of each of the response variables, if more than one response is to be studied:
   a. What form (type and degree) of model equation is most appropriate? Is the form of the model known or is it to be determined?
   b. Is an optimum value of the response sought, or if two or more responses are to be studied can a region which is optimal be found for all of the

responses simultaneously? If an optimum region for all responses is not possible, can we at least discover ''better'' conditions than our current operating conditions? Are we interested mainly in measuring the effects of the factors on each response?

    c. What is the expected magnitude of the experimental error variation (dispersion in the response values) in the test results? Is the magnitude of the dispersion different at different levels of the experimental factors?

iii. If a region of optimum values for several response(s) is sought, how shall we proceed in searching for the optimum?

iv. Finally, are we interested in describing the shape of the response surface in some well-defined neighborhood surrounding the optimum set of factor levels? How shall this be done?

Additional questions such as, ''Are there factor level conditions within the experimental region where the expected outcome is known or where the anticipated performance of the response variable is expected to be inferior?'' are sometimes asked. Also, ''What are the procedures for running a test, including the ease with which each of the factors can be changed from one test to the next?'' Such questions and others are outlined by Hahn (1984).

2

In this section we shall outline some basic methods for efficient experimentation which have proved useful in the planning of experiments and their sequential execution. These methods are designed to assist in

1. The selection of the *best model* among the set of plausible models.
2. The *efficient estimation* of the parameters (coefficients) in the selected model.

Both objectives are sought simultaneously and usually sequentially, because the experimenter generally does not know exactly what variables to measure, nor their range, nor what series of experiments to run until the experimental program is at least partially completed. In practice, one or more experiments are planned and carried out, the results analyzed, and the experimental plan is modified. Such a strategy was first introduced by Box and Wilson (1951).

The first step in the experimental strategy of RSM is to decide on a model form which expresses the response as a function of the independent variables in the process. This model provides the basis for new experimentation, which in turn may lead to a new model, and the entire cycle is repeated. Conclusions can be drawn from the first experiments. The experimentation can be terminated any time further experimentation appears uneconomical. Finally, the sequential fitting of models and the eventual selection of a model is a prelude to the determination of optimum operating conditions for a process.

Before discussing the fitting of first-order polynomials which constitutes the first step in the sequential model fitting procedure, a brief review of the method of least squares which will be used throughout this booklet for estimating the parameters in the models is necessary.

2.0 The Determination of Optimum Conditions

2.1 Least Squares Estimation of a Response Surface Model

Much of the analytical work in RSM deals with concepts centered around the general linear model. In Section 1.1.4 the polynomial representation of a response surface was introduced by saying that it could be written as a first-degree model in k variables of the form

$$Y_u = \beta_0 + \sum_{i=1}^{k} \beta_i X_{ui} + \epsilon_u \qquad u = 1, 2, \ldots, N. \tag{7}$$

In (7), Y_u is the observed value of η in the uth trial, X_{ui} is the value (or level) of the ith controllable factor in the uth trial, β_0 and β_i, $i = 1, 2, \ldots, k$, represent unknown parameters to be estimated, and ϵ_u is the error made when observing Y_u. If the first-degree model is not adequate, then the following can be used

$$Y_u = \beta_0 + \sum_{i=1}^{k} \beta_i X_{ui} + \sum_{i=1}^{k} \beta_{ii} X_{ui}^2 + \sum\sum_{i<j}^{k} \beta_{ij} X_{ui} X_{uj} + \epsilon_u \tag{8}$$

which is a model of the second degree. In this booklet, it will be assumed that the form, ϕ, of the surface can be approximated reasonably well by either a first-degree polynomial (7) or a second-degree polynomial (8).

The first step in fitting a model to approximate the response surface consists of collecting data and estimating the $k + 1$ unknown coefficients β_0 and β_i in equation 7 or the $(k + 1)(k + 2)/2$ unknown coefficients in Equation 8. After the coefficients are estimated, the estimates are then substituted into the equation resulting in the estimated response equation of Section 1.1.5. For estimating the coefficients, the following assumptions are made regarding the random errors ϵ_u in (7) or (8):

(a) the random errors ϵ_u have a *zero mean* and a *common variance σ^2*
(b) the random errors are *mutually independent* in the statistical sense.

For the usual tests of significance (t and F tests) and confidence interval estimation procedures, an additional assumption must be satisfied,

(c) the random errors ϵ_u are *normally distributed*.

To facilitate the estimation of the coefficients in the models (7) and (8), the variables in the models are reexpressed as coded variables. The most commonly used coding scheme is to define the coded variables, x_i, in standardized form as

$$x_{ui} = \frac{X_{ui} - \bar{X}_i}{S_i} \qquad i = 1, 2, \ldots, k \tag{9}$$

where $\bar{X}_i$ is the mean of the X_{ui} values ($u = 1, 2, \ldots, N$) and S_i is some scale factor. For example, if each of the k factors is to be set at two levels only (X_{LOW} and X_{HIGH}, say) and the same number of observations is to be collected at each level, then $\bar{X}_i = (X_{LOW} + X_{HIGH})/2$ and $S_i = (X_{HIGH} - X_{LOW})/2$. In this case the values of the coded variable x_{ui} in (9) are $x_{ui} = -1$ when $X_{ui} = X_{LOW}$ and $x_{ui} = +1$ when $X_{ui} = X_{HIGH}$. [The coding scheme of (9) produces the familiar ∓ 1 notation for the factor levels associated with two-level factorial arrangements (see Section 3.1).] Expressed in the coded variables, equations (7) and (8) are

$$Y_u = \beta_0 + \sum_{i=1}^{k} \beta_i x_{ui} + \epsilon_u \tag{10}$$

$$Y_u = \beta_0 + \sum_{i=1}^{k} \beta_i x_{ui} + \sum_{i=1}^{k} \beta_{ii} x_{ui}^2 + \sum\sum_{i<j}^{k} \beta_{ij} x_{ui} x_{uj} + \epsilon_u. \qquad (11)$$

Returning to the estimation of the coefficients $\beta_0, \beta_1, \beta_2, \ldots$ which are now expressed in models (10) and (11), when the assumptions (a) and (b) concerning the errors, ϵ_u, are satisfied, the *method of least squares* selects as the estimates $b_0, b_1, b_2, \ldots$ for the unknown coefficients, those values which minimize the quantity

$$R(\beta_0, \beta_1, \ldots) = \sum_{u=1}^{N} (Y_u - \beta_0 - \beta_1 x_{u1} - \ldots)^2$$

(Hereafter the unknown coefficients will be denoted by β and their estimates by b.) For a review of the method of least squares as well as a review of the properties of the least squares estimates using matrix notation, the reader is referred to appendix A.

The first-degree polynomial in k coded variables

$$Y_u = \beta_0 + \beta_1 x_{u1} + \beta_2 x_{u2} + \cdots + \beta_k x_{uk} + \epsilon_u \qquad (12)$$

2.2 The First-Degree Polynomial

is the simplest form (lowest-degree) of equation that is used. The model (12) is appropriate when:

(a) the interest is in studying the response behavior only within a *limited region* of the space of the k factors and where the range of response values can be approximated reasonably well by the hyperplane (12), and

(b) at the beginning stages of an experiment when it is not known what the shape of the surface is (that is, what degree polynomial is necessary to adequately model the response) nor where the location of the best response values are. In our search for the region of best response values, we begin with the simplest form of model in order to try to hold the number of experiments required as well as the cost of the experimentation to a minimum.

To estimate the coefficients in (12), data are required from only $N \geq k + 1$ distinct experimental trials. Designs used for fitting the first-degree model (12) are presented in Section 3. For the present assume that data are collected at the 2^k points of a two-level factorial arrangement in k variables where Y_u represents the observed response value for the uth trial, and the two levels of each coded x_i in (12) are denoted by -1 and $+1$. [The 2^k factorial arrangement is one of the simplest classes of designs and evolves from the desire to look only at two levels of each factor.] Then the estimates $b_0, b_1, \ldots, b_k$ of the coefficients in (12) are calculated using the simple formulas

$$b_0 = \frac{1}{N} \sum_{u=1}^{N} Y_u = \bar{Y}$$

$$b_i = \frac{\sum\limits_{u=1}^{N} x_{ui} Y_u}{\sum\limits_{u=1}^{N} x_{ui}^2} = \frac{1}{N} \sum_{u=1}^{N} x_{ui} Y_u \qquad i = 1, 2, \ldots, k \tag{13}$$

since $\sum\limits_{u=1}^{N} x_{ui}^2 = N$ is the sum of a series of squared ± 1s. If only a single observation is collected at each of the 2^k points, then $N = 2^k$; otherwise if replicates are collected at one or more points, then $N > 2^k$. With each of the k factors having two levels only, the estimates b_i, $i = 1, 2 \ldots, k$ are equal to half the estimated factorial effects given by the difference between the average responses at the $+1$ and -1 settings of the x_{ui}s. In other words, in (13) b_i can be expressed as

$$b_i = \tfrac{1}{2}[\bar{Y}_{x_i = +1} - \bar{Y}_{x_i = -1}]$$

where $\bar{Y}_{x_i = +1}$ and $\bar{Y}_{x_i = -1}$ are the average responses at $x_i = +1$ and $x_i = -1$, respectively. Furthermore, the variance of b_0 and of the b_i is

$$\mathrm{Var}(b_0) = \mathrm{Var}(b_i) = \frac{\sigma^2}{\sum\limits_{u=1}^{N} x_{ui}^2} = \frac{\sigma^2}{N} \qquad i = 1, 2, \ldots, k \tag{14}$$

where σ^2 is the variance of a single observation Y_u. It is interesting to note at this point that the $k + 1$ coefficient estimates have the same variance. This is a property of the 2^k factorial design. These designs are discussed in more detail in Section 3.1.

Once the estimates in (13) are obtained, they are then substituted into Equation 12 to produce the fitted model

$$\hat{Y} = b_0 + b_1 x_1 + b_2 x_2 + \cdots + b_k x_k. \tag{15}$$

Upon ascertaining the fitted model accounts for a significant amount of the variability in the observed response values (as discussed in Section 2.5 on testing for lack of fit), the model (15) is then referred to as a *prediction equation* or *estimation equation*. Predicted values of the response are obtained using (15) by selecting values for $X_1, X_2, \ldots, X_k$, calculating the coded values of $x_1, x_2, \ldots, x_k$ using (9), and then by substituting the calculated values of the coded variables into (15).

An example consisting of two independent factors ($k = 2$) will be worked through to illustrate how to calculate the coefficient estimates and their variances and to estimate the surface with a model of the form (15).

2.3 An Example of a Fitted First-Degree Polynomial

The surface abrasion resistance (or hardness) of manufactured plastic disks was presumed to be related to the composition of the disks as well as the position location of the disk in the mold. Disk composition was measured as the ratio of the concentrations of filler (f) to epoxy resin (e) so that $\xi_1 = f/e$. The position (ξ_2) of the disk in the model was measured in units of distance (centimeters) from a reference point. The measured response for each plastic disk is the thickness of the disk (in units of millimeters) after subjecting the disk to 5000 cycles of an abrasion test. The disks were assumed to be of uniform thickness prior to subjecting them to the abrasion test. Ultimately, the objective of the study is to find the values of ξ_1 and ξ_2 that produce disks exhibiting the least amount of wear.

Two levels of composition ratio ($X_1 = 5/8$ and $7/8$) and two position values ($X_2 = 1.5$ and 2.5 cm) were selected for the experiment. At each of the four factor-level combinations a single plastic disk was produced. The four combinations were replicated twice producing eight disks in all, two per combination. The sequence of factor-level combinations for producing the disks was $(X_1, X_2) = (5/8, 2.5), (7/8, 1.5), (7/8, 2.5), (5/8, 1.5), (7/8, 1.5), (5/8, 2.5), (7/8, 2.5)$, and $(5/8, 1.5)$. The observed thickness values of the eight disks after 5000 abrasion cycles and the values of the coded variables x_1 and x_2 are listed in Table 1. The coded variables are defined as $x_1 = (X_1 - 3/4)/(1/8)$ and $x_2 = (X_2 - 2.0)/0.5$. The location of the four-point design relative to the overall region of possible factor-level combinations is shown in Figure 3.

The model to be fitted to the disk thickness values is

$$Y = \beta_0 + \beta_1 x_1 + \beta_2 x_2 + \epsilon. \tag{16}$$

Referring to the formulas (13) for calculating the estimates b_0, b_1, and b_2, the following is found

$$b_0 = \frac{1}{8} (7.0 + 6.9 + 5.2 + \cdots + 5.8) = \frac{1}{8} (50.7) = 6.3375$$

$$b_1 = \frac{1}{8} [(-1)7.0 + (-1)6.9 + (-1)5.2 + \cdots + (+1)5.8]$$

$$= \frac{1}{8} (-24 + 26.2) = 0.2125$$

or

$$b_1 = \frac{1}{2}(\bar{Y}_{x_1=+1} - \bar{Y}_{x_1=-1}) = \frac{1}{2}(6.550 - 6.125)$$

$$b_2 = \frac{1}{2}(5.625 - 7.050) = -0.7125.$$

Table 1
Plastic Disk Thickness Values at Each of the Four Factor Combinations

Original Factors		Coded Variables			Thickness
Composition ($X_1 = f/e$)	Position (X_2)	x_1	x_2	Point	(Y = millimeters)
5/8	1.5	−1	−1	1.	7.0, 6.9
5/8	2.5	−1	+1	2.	5.2, 5.4
7/8	1.5	+1	−1	3.	7.1, 7.2
7/8	2.5	+1	+1	4.	6.1, 5.8

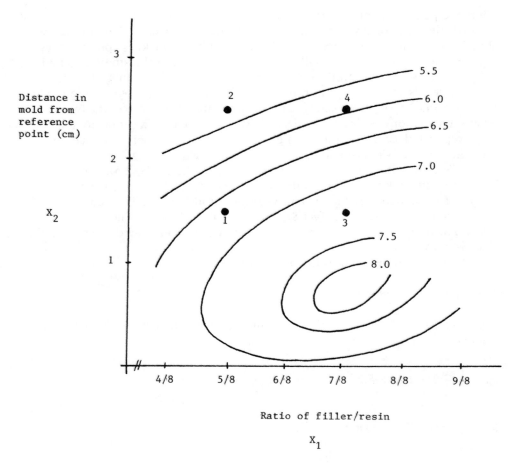

Figure 3
Contours of the unknown disk thickness surface and the initial
experimental design

The variance of the estimated coefficients is, from (14), $\text{Var}(b_0) = \text{Var}(b_i) = \sigma^2/8$. Upon substituting the values of the estimated coefficients into (16), the fitted first-degree model is

$$\hat{Y} = 6.3375 + 0.2125x_1 - 0.7125x_2 \qquad (17)$$
$$\quad (0.0484) \quad (0.0484) \quad (0.0484)$$

where the quantities in parentheses below the coefficient estimates are the estimated standard errors of the coefficient estimates. The estimated standard errors are the positive square roots of the estimated variances of the coefficient estimates, that is, $\sqrt{s^2/8}$, where s^2 is an estimate of σ^2, and is calculated from the pair of replicated disks at each of the four composition-position combinations.

The formula for s^2 is $\sum_{i=1}^{n} d_i^2/2n$, where d_i is the difference between the pair of response values at the ith design point and $i = 1, 2, \ldots, n = 4$. From the entries in Table 1, the value of s^2 is $s^2 = [(7.0 - 6.9)^2 + (5.2 - 5.4)^2 + (7.1 - 7.2)^2 + (6.1 - 5.8)^2]/(8) = 0.01875$ so that $\sqrt{0.01875/8} = 0.0484$. [An alternate estimate of σ^2 is the residual mean square taken from the analysis of variance table. We shall discuss in the next section how to set up the analysis of variance table.]

Thus far in this example a fitted first-degree model using the disk thickness values of Table 1 has been obtained as well as an estimate of σ^2 from the replicated disks at each combination of the levels of ξ_1 and ξ_2. Before inferring what the effects are of disk composition (ξ_1) and position in the mold (ξ_2) from the estimates b_1 and b_2 in the model (17), it must be determined that the fitted model explains a sufficient amount of the total variation in the measured response values to have confidence in it. The appropriateness of the fitted model is determined by setting up an analysis of variance table and then comparing certain entries in the table to one another. This will be discussed now.

2.4 The Analysis of Variance Table for Testing the Significance of the Coefficient Estimates in the Fitted Model

The results of the analysis of a set of experimental data can be displayed in table form known as the *analysis of variance table*. The entries in the table represent sources that contribute to the total variation in the data values.

The total variation in the data values is called the "total sum of squares," SST, and is computed by summing the squares of the observed Y_us about their average value $\bar{Y} = (Y_1 + Y_2 + \cdots + Y_N)/N$,

$$\text{SST} = \sum_{u=1}^{N} (Y_u - \bar{Y})^2. \tag{18}$$

The quantity SST has associated with it N-1 degrees of freedom.

The total sum of squares is the sum of two quantities; the sum of squares due to regression (or accounted for by the fitted model) plus the sum of squares not accounted for by the fitted model. The formula for the sum of squares due to regression of the fitted model containing p terms is

$$\text{SSR} = \sum_{u=1}^{N} (\hat{Y}_u - \bar{Y})^2 \tag{19}$$

where the deviation $\hat{Y}_u - \bar{Y}$ represents a measure of the difference between the value predicted by the fitted model ($\hat{Y}_u$) for the uth observed value and the overall average of the Y_us. The degrees of freedom associated with SSR is the number of terms in the fitted model minus one, p-1.

The sum of squares not accounted for by the fitted regression model is

$$\text{SSE} = \sum_{u=1}^{N} (Y_u - \bar{Y}_u)^2 \tag{20}$$

which is also called the *sum of squares of the residuals*. The degrees of freedom for SSE is N-p which is the difference (N-1) − (p-1) = N-p.

Table 2
The Analysis of Variance Table

Source	df	Sum of Squares	Mean Square
Due to Regression (fitted model)	p-1	SSR	SSR/(p-1)
Residual	N-p	SSE	SSE/(N-p)
Total	N-1	SST	

The analysis of variance table displaying the total, regression, and residual sums of squares (as well as the mean squares) is shown in Table 2.

The usual *test of significance of the fitted regression equation* is a test of the null hypothesis H_0: All of the βs (excluding β_0) are zero against the alternative hypothesis H_A: At least one of the βs (excluding β_0) is not zero. The test, assuming normality of the errors, involves the F statistic

$$F = \frac{\text{Mean Square Regression}}{\text{Mean Square Residual}} = \frac{\text{SSR}/(p\text{-}1)}{\text{SSE}/(N\text{-}p)}. \qquad (21)$$

If the null hypothesis is true, the F-ratio in (21) follows an F distribution with p-1 and N-p degrees of freedom in the numerator and in the denominator, respectively. The value of F in (21) is compared to the table value $F_{(p\text{-}1,N\text{-}p,\alpha)}$, which is the upper 100α percent point of the F distribution with p-1 and N-p degrees of freedom, respectively. If the value of F in (21) exceeds $F_{(p\text{-}1,N\text{-}p,\alpha)}$, then the null hypothesis is rejected at the α level of significance and it is inferred that the coefficient estimates are not all zero (that is, one or more convey information about the surface) and the variation accounted for by the model (through the b_is, $i \neq 0$) is significantly greater than the unexplained variation.

An accompanying statistic to the F statistic of equation 21 that is often calculated in the analysis of a fitted model is

$$R^2 = \frac{\text{SSR}}{\text{SST}}. \qquad (22)$$

The value of R^2 is a measure of the "proportion of total variation of the Y_us about the mean $\bar{Y}$ explained by the fitted regression equation." It is often expressed as a percentage by multiplying the ratio SSR/SST by 100%. One drawback to using R^2 as a criterion of model adequacy is that as the number of parameters estimated in the model approaches the number of observations in the data set (that is, when there are no replicate observations), the value of R^2 will approach one even if the model is not appropriate.

A related statistic, called the adjusted R^2 statistic is preferred over R^2 by some workers and is

$$R_A^2 = 1 - \frac{\text{SSE}/(N\text{-}p)}{\text{SST}/(N\text{-}1)}$$
$$= 1 - (1\text{-}R)^2 \left(\frac{N\text{-}1}{N\text{-}p}\right). \qquad (23)$$

An adjustment to R^2 has been made in (23) by using the degrees of freedom corresponding to SSE and SST. The R_A^2 statistic is a measure of the drop in the

Table 3
Observed and Predicted Disk Thickness Values at Each of the Four Design Points as Well as Relevant Differences for Calculating the Sums of Squares

x_1	x_2	Y_u	$\hat{Y}_u$	$Y_u - \bar{Y}$	$\hat{Y}_u - \bar{Y}$	$Y_u - \hat{Y}_u$
-1	-1	7.0	6.8375	0.6625	0.5000	0.1625
-1	-1	6.9	6.8375	0.5625	0.5000	0.0625
-1	$+1$	5.2	5.4125	-1.1375	-0.9250	-0.2125
-1	$+1$	5.4	5.4125	-0.9375	-0.9250	-0.0125
$+1$	-1	7.1	7.2625	0.7625	0.9250	-0.1625
$+1$	-1	7.2	7.2625	0.8625	0.9250	-0.0625
$+1$	$+1$	6.1	5.8375	-0.2375	-0.5000	0.2625
$+1$	$+1$	5.8	5.8375	-0.5375	-0.5000	-0.0375
		$\Sigma Y_u = 50.7$		$\Sigma(Y_u - \bar{Y})^2 =$	$\Sigma(\hat{Y}_u - \bar{Y})^2 =$	$\Sigma(Y_u - \hat{Y}_u)^2 =$
		$\bar{Y} = 6.3375$		4.59875	4.4225	0.17625

magnitude of the estimate of the error variance achieved by fitting a model other than $Y = \beta_0 + \epsilon$ relative to the estimate of the error variance that would be obtained by fitting the model $Y = \beta_0 + \epsilon$.

To illustrate the sums of squares calculations for the entries in the analysis of variance table, refer to the plastic disk thickness values in Table 1 and to the fitted model (17). Table 3 lists the observed disk thickness values, the estimates ($\hat{Y}_u$) obtained with the fitted model (17), and the differences $Y_u - \bar{Y}$, $\hat{Y}_u - \bar{Y}$, and $Y_u - \hat{Y}_u$. At the bottom of Table 3 are the quantities SST = 4.59875, SSR = 4.4225, and SSE = 0.17625.

Table 4
Analysis of Variance of Disk Thickness Values

Source	df	SS	Mean Square	F	R^2	R_A^2
Due to Regression (fitted model)	2	4.42250	2.21125	62.73	0.9617	0.9463
Residual	5	0.17625	0.03525			
Total	7	4.59875				

The analysis of variance table, Table 2, along with the computed F, R^2 and R_A^2 values is shown in Table 4 where the values of F, R^2, and R_A^2 were obtained as follows,

$$F = \frac{\text{MS Due to Regression}}{\text{MS Residual}} = \frac{2.21125}{0.03525} = 62.73$$

$$R^2 = \frac{\text{SS Due to Regression}}{\text{SS Total}} = \frac{4.42250}{4.59875} = 0.9617$$

$$R_A^2 = 1 - \frac{\text{MS Residual}}{\text{SS Total}/7} = 1 - \frac{0.03525}{4.59875/7} = 0.9463.$$

Since the value $F = 62.73$ exceeds the table value $F_{(2,5,.01)} = 13.27$, the null hypothesis is rejected that states both β_1 and β_2 in (16) are zero and infer that one or both are nonzero. Similarly, the values of the accompanying statistics $R^2 = 0.9617$ and $R_A^2 = 0.9463$ show that $100\%(R^2) = 96.17\%$ of the total variation is explained by the fitted model (17), and the estimate of the error variance, provided by the residual mean square (after fitting the model (17)), is only $100\%(1-R_A^2) = 5.37\%$ of the error variance estimate that would have been obtained using the total mean square (that is, using the model $\hat{Y} = \bar{Y}$).

The rejection of the hypothesis H_0: all β_i (excluding β_0) are zero is not the same as saying the fitted model adequately describes the behavior of the response over the experimental region; rather, rejecting H_0 implies that not all of the β_i are zero. A procedure for testing the adequacy of the fitted model is called *testing lack of fit* of the fitted model and this test will be discussed now.

2.5 How to Test for Lack of Fit of a First-Degree Polynomial

Lack of fit of the fitted first-degree model

$$\hat{Y} = b_0 + \sum_{i=1}^{k} b_i x_i \tag{24}$$

can result from the presence of *nonplanarity* or possibly from a curvature in the shape of *the response surface* which goes undetected owing to the exclusion of pure quadratic (or cubic) terms in (24) such as $b_{ii}x_i^2$ (or $b_{iii}x_i^3$) or from the presence of *interaction effects* among the experimental factors (ξ_i and ξ_j), which also is undetectable owing to the exclusion of crossproduct terms in (24) such as $b_{ij}x_i x_j$ or $b_{ijk}x_i x_j x_k$. In both cases, in fitting a model of the form (24) and in describing the estimated surface as being a hyperplane, the complexity of the response surface has been understated and as such an error in judgment regarding the effects of the experimental factors on the behavior of the response has occurred.

The test for lack of fit of the model (24) requires the following two conditions of the experimental design to be satisfied:

i. the number of distinct design points, *n, must exceed the number of terms in the fitted model,* that is, $n > k + 1$, and

ii. *at least 2 replicate observations* must be collected at one or more of the design points in order to calculate an estimate of the error variance unless, of course, one has an estimate of the error variance from previous experiments.

In addition, the random errors (ϵ_u) will be assumed to be normal and independently distributed with a common variance σ^2.

When conditions (i) and (ii) hold, the residual sum of squares, SSE of equation 20, consists of two sources of variation. The first source is due to lack of fit of the fitted model (which is assumed to be due to the exclusion of higher order terms in [24]) and the other source is pure error variation. To partition the residual sum of squares into these sources, first the sum of squares due to the replicate observations is calculated from the replicates. This is called *pure error sum of squares* (or SS Pure Error). The lack of fit sum of squares is obtained by subtracting the pure error sum of squares from the residual sum of squares.

To illustrate the partitioning of the residual sum of squares, denote the uth observation at the lth design point by Y_{lu}, where $u = 1, 2, \ldots, r_l \geq 1$, and $l = 1, 2, \ldots, n$. Define $\bar{Y}_l$ to be the average of the r_l observations at the lth design point. Then,

$$\text{SS Pure Error} = \sum_{l=1}^{n} \sum_{u=1}^{r_l} (Y_{lu} - \bar{Y}_l)^2 \tag{25}$$

and

$$\text{SS Lack of Fit} = \text{SSE} - \text{SS Pure Error}$$

$$= \sum_{l=1}^{n} r_l(\hat{Y}_l - \bar{Y}_l)^2 \tag{26}$$

where $\hat{Y}_l$ is the predicted value of the response at the lth design point produced by the fitted model (24). Furthermore, the degrees of freedom associated with SS Pure Error is

$$\sum_{l=1}^{n} (r_l - l) = \text{N-n}$$

where N is the total number of observations collected at the n design points, so that the degrees of freedom associated with SS Lack of Fit is obtained by subtraction and is $(\text{N-p}) - (\text{N-n}) = \text{n-p}$, where $p = k + 1$ is the number of terms in (24).

The *test of adequacy of the fitted model* is

$$F = \frac{\text{SS Lack of Fit/(n-p)}}{\text{SS Pure Error/(N-n)}}. \tag{27}$$

The hypothesis of adequacy of fit is rejected at the α level of significance when the calculated value of F in (27) is larger than the table value of $F_{(\text{n-p},\text{N-n},\alpha)}$. When the calculated value is not larger than the table value, then the residual mean square is used as an estimate of σ^2 and is also used to test the significance of the fitted model.

When the hypothesis of adequacy of fit is rejected, the first-degree model is upgraded by the addition of crossproduct terms and/or higher-degree terms in x_1, $x_2, \ldots, x_k$. If additional design points are required in order to estimate all of the coefficients in the revised model form, these points are added. Then data are collected from these points and the analysis is redone.

To illustrate the test for lack of fit of the first-degree model (17) that was fitted to the disk thickness values in Table 1, refer to the analysis of variance shown in Table 4. This table displays the partitioning of the total variation in the eight disk thickness values into the variation accounted for by the fitted model (Regression) and the variation that is not accounted for by the fitted model (Residual). Further, note that the magnitude of the residual sum of squares is $\text{SSE} = 0.17625$ with 5 degrees of freedom. The replicated disk thickness values at each combination of the levels of x_1 and x_2 are used to calculate the sum of squares for pure error using (25). Thus,

$$\text{SS Pure Error} = [(7.0 - 6.95)^2 + (6.9 - 6.95)^2 + (5.2 - 5.3)^2 + \cdots + (5.8 - 5.95)^2]$$

$$= 0.075 \text{ with 4 df} \tag{28}$$

where 6.95 is the average thickness value at point 1, 5.3 is the average at point 2, and so on. From (26),

$$SS \text{ Lack of Fit} = SSE - SS \text{ Pure Error}$$
$$= 0.17625 - 0.075$$
$$= 0.10125 \text{ with } 5 - 4 = 1 \text{ df}$$

To test the adequacy of the fitted model (17) using (27), calculate

$$F = \frac{0.10125/1}{0.075/4} = 5.4 \qquad (29)$$

and since $F = 5.4$ does not exceed $F_{(1,4,.05)} = 7.71$, the hypothesis of adequacy of fit cannot be rejected and it can be inferred that the surface is a plane. In passing, the test for lack of fit (29) is equivalent to having fitted the model $Y = \beta_0 + \beta_1 x_1 + \beta_2 x_2 + \beta_{12} x_1 x_2 + \epsilon$ and tested the hypothesis $H_0: \beta_{12} = 0$ vs $H_A: \beta_{12} = 0$. If $H_0: \beta_{12} = 0$ is rejected, this test for nonplanarity would imply the surface exhibits a twisted shape.

The fitting of a first-degree model to data collected at the points of a first-order design (the 2^k factorial arrangement) has been discussed. How to test for the goodness of fit of the model in fitting the observed response values at the design points has also been discussed. Having decided that the fitted first-degree model accurately describes the response surface, it can be used to search for levels of the controllable variables ($\xi_1, \xi_2, \ldots, \xi_k$) that would produce more optimal values of the response. That is to say, the first-degree model will now be used

$$\hat{Y} = 6.3375 + 0.2125 x_1 - 0.7125 x_2 \qquad (30)$$

to search for other values of disk composition (ξ_1) and disk position in the mold (ξ_2) that produce harder disks with greater resistance to the abrasion tests (i.e., higher values of Y). The ultimate objective is to find the *specific combination of the values of ξ_1 and ξ_2 that produce disks, which when subjected to the abrasion test, exhibit the least amount of wear.*

In search for values of ξ_1 and ξ_2 that produce thicker disks, first take notice of the signs and magnitudes of the coefficient estimates $b_1 = 0.2125$ and $b_2 = -0.7125$, respectively, in model (30). Since $b_1 > 0$ and $b_2 < 0$, thicker disks are naturally expected to result by raising the ratio of the filler to epoxy resin ($\xi_1 = f/e$) and by moving the position of the disk closer to the reference point in the mold. This decision is supported also by what is referred to by Hunter (1959a) as "*mapping the surface.*"

2.6 Mapping the Surface: Plotting Surface Contours

The fitted model $\hat{Y} = 6.3375 + 0.2125 x_1 - 0.7125 x_2$ can now be used to "map" empirically the response function over the experimental region. This mapping takes the form of a contour plot (see Section 1.1.7) of the estimated surface as shown in Figure 4. The contour lines are drawn by connecting two points (coordinate settings of x_1 and x_2) in the experimental region that produce the same value

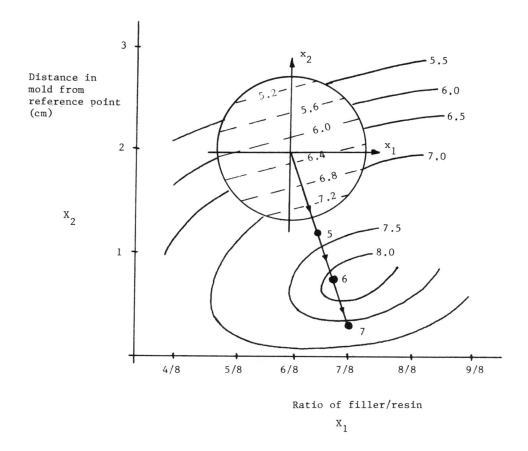

Figure 4
The best fitting plane and the estimated path of steepest ascent

of $\hat{Y}$. For example, when $\hat{Y} = 6.2$ is substituted in the fitted equation, the result is the equation of a straight line; that is, $0.1375 + 0.2125x_1 - 0.7125x_2 = 0$. If we set $x_1 = 0$, then solving for x_2 the following is obtained

$$x_2 = \frac{0.1375}{0.7125} = 0.193.$$

If we now set $x_2 = 0$, then solving for x_1 the following is obtained

$$x_1 = \frac{-0.1375}{0.2125} = -0.647.$$

The contour line for $\hat{Y} = 6.2$ passes through the coordinate settings $(x_1, x_2) = (0, 0.193)$ and $(-0.647, 0)$, and is drawn to extend slightly beyond the boundaries of the experimental region defined by $x_1 = \pm1$ and $x_2 = \pm1$.

The direction of tilt of the estimated disk thickness planar surface is indicated by the direction of the arrow which is drawn perpendicular to the surface contour lines in Figure 4. Since the arrow points downward and to the right, this means that higher values of the response (thicker disk values) are expected with decreasing values of x_2 and with increasing values of x_1. This corresponds to moving the position of the disk in the mold closer to the reference point as well as increasing the ratio of filler to epoxy resin. These recommendations comprise the beginning steps in a series of experiments to be performed along the *path of steepest ascent* up the surface.

2.6.1 The Path of Steepest Ascent

Starting at the center (0, 0) of the experimental design, the direction of the path of steepest ascent is to simultaneously move b_1 (= +0.2125) units in the x_1 direction for every b_2 (= −0.7125) units in the x_2 direction. The sizes of the step changes in the x_1 and x_2 directions depend on the particular units that were used in scaling the original factor levels, X_1 and X_2, in defining the coded variables, x_1 and x_2. In this example, the scaling units were 1/8 and 1/2, for x_1 and x_2, respectively. Different scaling units would have resulted in a different direction for the path. For further reading on what effect the size of the scale units has on the "direction of steepest ascent" the reader is directed to the discussion of the paper by Box and Wilson (1951), in particular, the comments by N. L. Johnson, and to Khuri and Cornell (1987), Chapter 5.

Experiments are now performed along the path of steepest ascent at points 5, 6, and 7, as illustrated in Figure 4. At these points, the values of X_1 and X_2 and the observed disk thickness values are

Point	X_1	X_2	Y
5	13/16	1.16	7.4
6	27/32	0.74	8.3
7	14/16	0.32	7.1

Upon viewing an increase in the response value at points 5 and 6, compared to the previous 8 observed values collected during the initial set of experiments, followed by a decrease at point 7, at this moment either the ratio of filler to resin is too high at 14/16 or 7/8 or the position in the mold of 0.32 cm from the reference point is too close, and additional experimentation along the path would not be beneficial. Instead, retreat back to point 6 and perform a second set of experiments. The center of the second design will be taken at point 6 where the settings of X_1 and X_2 are $X_1 = 27/32$ and $X_2 = 0.74$ or 0.75.

A second 2^2 factorial arrangement was set up with point 6 as the center. The coded variables, x_1 and x_2, are defined as

$$x_1 = \frac{X_1 - 27/32}{3/32}, \qquad x_2 = \frac{X_2 - 0.75}{0.25} \tag{31}$$

where the scale unit 3/32 for x_1 is slightly less than the first design and the scale unit (0.25) for x_2 is one-half the size used previously. The levels of composition and position in mold, the experiment design levels, and the observed thickness

Table 5
Disk Thickness Values for the Second 2^2 Factorial with Center
Point Replicates

Composition (X_1)	Position (X_2)	Coded Variables		Thickness (Y)
		x_1	x_2	
12/16	0.50	−1	−1	7.3
12/16	1.00	−1	1	7.1
15/16	0.50	1	−1	7.0
15/16	1.00	1	1	8.0
27/32	0.75	0	0	8.2
27/32	0.75	0	0	8.3

values are listed in Table 5 and are shown in Figure 5. A second replicate of the center point (point 6) was performed so that when compared to the thickness value of 8.3 collected previously at point 6, an estimate of the pure error variation could be obtained.

The first-degree model fitted to the disk thickness values in Table 5 is

$$\hat{Y} = 7.65 + 0.15x_1 + 0.20x_2 \tag{32}$$

and the analysis of variance table, complete with the entries for lack of fit and pure error, is

Source	df	SS	Mean Square	F
Regression	2	0.250	0.125	
Residual	3	1.445	0.482	
Lack of Fit	2	1.440	0.720	144
Pure Error	1	0.005	0.005	
Total	5	1.695		

The F test for lack of fit which is based on only 2 and 1 degrees of freedom in the numerator and denominator, respectively, and as such is not a very powerful test, moderately suggests the fitted model (32) is not adequate. This comes as no surprise when noticing the high thickness values at the center of the design in relation to the thickness values at the 2^2 design points. To circumvent the problem of too few degrees of freedom for the estimate of the pure error variance in the denominator of the F test, pool the previous estimate in (28), $s^2 = 0.01875$ with 4 degrees of freedom, in with the present estimate $s^2 = 0.005$ with one degree of freedom. The pooled estimate would then be

$$s^2_{\text{pooled}} = \frac{4(0.01875) + 1(0.005)}{4 + 1} = 0.016.$$

The F test for lack of fit now becomes

$$F = \frac{0.720}{0.016} = 45.0 > F_{(2,5,.01)} = 13.27$$

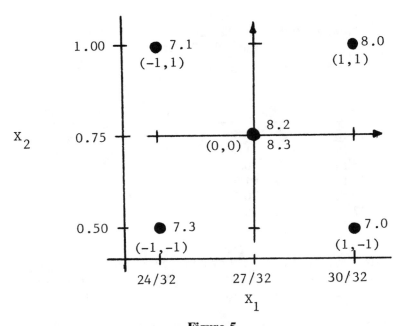

Figure 5
A 2^2 factorial design with replicated center point. Numbers in parentheses represent design coordinate settings (x_1, x_2) in the coded variables x_1 and x_2

which is highly significant. Pooling estimates of variance is valid whenever good reasons exist to support the belief that the error variance has not changed from one set of experiments to another.

When the hypothesis of adequacy of fit is rejected, the first-degree model is upgraded by the addition of crossproduct terms and/or higher-degree terms in x_1, $x_2, \ldots, x_k$. If additional design points are required to estimate all of the coefficients in the revised model form, these points are added, data are collected from these points, and the analysis is redone.

A simple test for *surface curvature* is now described that can be performed by augmenting any first-order design with center point replicates. Such a test is called *"a single degree of freedom test for surface curvature."*

2.6.2 The Single Degree of Freedom Test for Surface Curvature: Replicating Center Point Observations

Suppose observed values of the response are collected at the n_1 points of a first-order design (either a 2^k factorial arrangement or a simplex design consisting of $n_1 = k + 1$ points as will be described in Section 3). Denote the average of the n_1 observations by $\bar{Y}_{n_1}$. Suppose further, that $n_0 > 1$ replicate observations are collected at the center of the design where the center point is defined by the coordinate settings $(x_1, x_2, \ldots, x_k) = (0, 0, \ldots, 0)$. Denote the average of the center point replicate observations by $\bar{Y}_{n_0}$. Then a test for surface curvature is performed by calculating

$$F = \frac{(\bar{Y}_{n_1} - \bar{Y}_{n_0})^2}{s^2 \left(\dfrac{1}{n_1} + \dfrac{1}{n_0}\right)} \tag{33}$$

where s^2 is a measure of the sample variance calculated from the $n_0 > 1$ replicated observations at the center of the design, and by comparing the value of F in (33) to the tabled value of $F_{(1,n_0-1,\alpha)}$. Curvature in the surface is suspected when the value of F in (33) exceeds the tabled value. In the case of a significantly large F value, if one then wishes to obtain a specific measure of the surface curvature, additional terms such as $\beta_{ii}x_i^2$ and $\beta_{ij}x_ix_j$ are added to the first-degree model (10) and additional points are added to the factorial arrangement with center point replicates, as described in Section 4, to estimate the β_{ii}, $i = 1, 2, \ldots, k$.

Suppose replicate observations are collected at some of the design points also. Then s^2 in the denominator of (33) is calculated by pooling the estimate of the error variance obtained from each group of replicates at the design points with the sum of squares among the replicates at the center of the design and dividing by the pooled degrees of freedom. If this number of degrees of freedom is denoted by ν, then the table value of F for comparing the value of F in (33) is $F_{(1,\nu,\alpha)}$.

The test (33) for surface curvature is illustrated by referring to the response values in Figure 5. There are two ($n_0 = 2$) center point observations, 8.2 and 8.3, so that the average thickness value at the center is $\bar{Y}_2 = 8.25$. Averaging the thickness values at the 4 design points produces $\bar{Y}_4 = 7.35$. At the center of the design, the sum of squares of the deviations of each observation from $\bar{Y}_2 = 8.25$ is used to calculate s^2,

$$s^2 = [(8.2 - 8.25)^2 + (8.3 - 8.25)^2]/1$$
$$= 0.005.$$

The value of the F test in (33) for testing the *presence of surface curvature* is

$$F = \frac{(7.35 - 8.25)^2}{0.005 \left(\dfrac{1}{4} + \dfrac{1}{2}\right)} = 216.0 > F_{(1,1,.10)} = 39.9$$

prompting us to suggest as the next step, the augmentation of the first-degree model by adding terms like $\beta_{11}x_1^2$, $\beta_{22}x_2^2$, and $\beta_{12}x_1x_2$ to it. The inclusion of the three terms to the first-degree polynomial produces the second-degree polynomial (11).

To estimate the coefficients of the separate terms in the second-degree model requires additional points be added to the centered 2^k factorial arrangement. After the second-degree fitted model has been checked for adequacy of fit and found to adequately fit the observed response values, then the next step in the surface investigation process is to perform a more detailed *"local"* exploration.

In the next two sections then the goals will be to:

i. *obtain an adequate model representation* of the estimated second-order response surface.
ii. use the model in (i) to locate the coordinates $(x_{01}, x_{02}, \ldots, x_{0k})$, of the *stationary point* which is where the slope of the estimated response surface (i) is equal to zero. If the stationary point is found to be inside the experimental region, then proceed to goal (iii). If the stationary point is not inside the region, then further experimentation taken in the direction of the stationary point is necessary.

iii. describe the *nature of the stationary point*. Is it a maximum, a minimum, or a saddle point (minimax point)?

Once these goals have been attained, then

iv. *describe the shape of the response surface* in the vicinity of the stationary point.

Before embarking on this plan of attack to reach the goals just listed, note that with the two-variable disk thickness example used up to this point there are basically only two types of response surfaces that can be encountered. It might be found that the stationary point is a maximum (it could be a minimum) or the stationary point is a minimax point (also called a saddle point). With a minimax point, the height of the estimated surface drops off as one moves away from the stationary point in one direction and the height increases as one moves away from the point in a direction perpendicular to the first direction. Often the presence of a minimax point indicates the presence of two distinct regions containing maximums, implying the existence of two distinct fundamental and different mechanisms.

2.7 Fitting a Second-Degree Model in the Neighborhood of the Optimal Response Value

Consider the fitting of a second-degree model in k variables of the form

$$Y = \beta_0 + \sum_{i=1}^{k} \beta_i x_i + \sum_{i=1}^{k} \beta_{ii} x_i^2 + \sum_{i<j}\sum \beta_{ij} x_i x_j + \epsilon \tag{34}$$

where the β_i are regression coefficients for the first-degree terms, the β_{ii} are coefficients for the pure quadratic terms, the β_{ij} are the coefficients for the cross-product terms, and ϵ is the random error term. The pure quadratic and crossproduct terms are of degree 2. The number of terms in the model of Equation 34 is $p = (k + 1)(k + 2)/2$; for example, when $k = 2$, then $p = 6$.

Designs which are used for collecting observed values of the response for estimating the coefficients in a second-degree model of the form (34) are presented in Section 4. For now, assume that observed response values are collected at the points of a second-order design and the fitted second-degree polynomial is

$$\hat{Y} = b_0 + \sum_{i=1}^{k} b_i x_i + \sum_{i=1}^{k} b_{ii} x_i^2 + \sum_{i<j}\sum b_{ij} x_i x_j. \tag{35}$$

After the fitted model of Equation 35 is checked for adequacy of fit in the region defined by the coordinates of the design and is found to be adequate, then proceed with the goals of locating the coordinates of the stationary point and of performing a more detailed analysis of the response system.

To illustrate the fitting of the second-degree model (35) where $k = 2$, suppose four additional design points are added to the centered 2^2 factorial design of Figure 5. The four extra design points (called axial points) are positioned on the x_1 and x_2 axes at the settings $(x_1, x_2) = (\pm\sqrt{2}, 0)$ and $(x_1, x_2) = (0, \pm\sqrt{2})$. The nine design settings are presented in Figures 6a and 6b, and comprise what is known as a

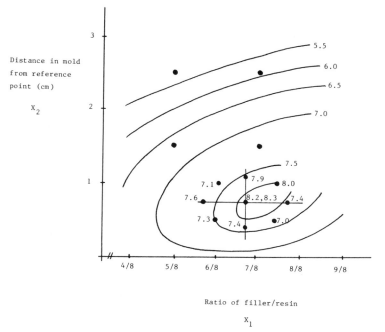

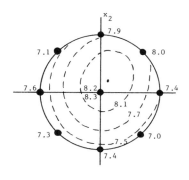

Figure 6a
A second-order design and the observed response values at the design points

Figure 6b
The central composite rotatable design in the coded variables x_1 and x_2 and contours (dotted curves) of the estimated disk thickness surface in the experimental region of the coded variables x_1 and x_2

central composite rotatable design (Section 4.2). Formulas for calculating the coefficient estimates in a second-order model using a central composite rotatable design are provided in Appendix B. The data for the complete experimental program are listed in Table 6.

Table 6
Observed Disk Thickness Values at the Points of a
Second-Order Design

Original Factor Levels		Coded Variables		Response Designation	Disk Thickness
X_1	X_2	x_1	x_2		
24/32 = .750	0.50	−1	−1	Y_1	7.3
24/32 = .750	1.00	−1	1	Y_2	7.1
30/32 = .9375	0.50	1	−1	Y_3	7.0
30/32 = .9375	1.00	1	1	Y_4	8.0
.711	0.75	$-\sqrt{2}$	0	Y_5	7.6
.977	0.75	$\sqrt{2}$	0	Y_6	7.4
27/32 = .844	0.396	0	$-\sqrt{2}$	Y_7	7.4
.844	1.104	0	$\sqrt{2}$	Y_8	7.9
.844	0.75	0	0	Y_9	8.2
.844	0.75	0	0	Y_{10}	8.3

The number of observations at the factorial, axial, and center point settings are $M = 4$, $2k = 4$, and $n_0 = 2$, respectively, so that the values of the coefficient estimates, using Equation B3 (see Appendix B) are

$$b_0 = \frac{1}{2}(Y_9 + Y_{10}) = 8.25$$

$$b_1 = \frac{1}{8}(-Y_1 - Y_2 + Y_3 + Y_4) + \frac{\sqrt{2}}{8}(Y_6 - Y_5) = 0.0396$$

$$b_2 = \frac{1}{8}(-Y_1 + Y_2 - Y_3 + Y_4) + \frac{\sqrt{2}}{8}(Y_8 - Y_7) = 0.1884$$

$$b_{11} = \frac{1}{16}\sum_{u=1}^{4} Y_u - \frac{1}{16}\sum_{u=5}^{8} Y_u - \frac{1}{4}(Y_9 + Y_{10}) + \frac{1}{4}(Y_5 + Y_6) = -0.4313$$

$$b_{22} = \frac{1}{16}\sum_{u=1}^{4} Y_u - \frac{1}{16}\sum_{u=5}^{8} Y_u - \frac{1}{4}(Y_9 + Y_{10}) + \frac{1}{4}(Y_7 + Y_8) = -0.3563$$

$$b_{12} = \frac{1}{4}(Y_1 - Y_2 - Y_3 + Y_4) = 0.300.$$

The fitted second-degree model is,

$$\hat{Y} = 8.25 + 0.0396x_1 + 0.1884x_2 - 0.4313x_1^2 - 0.3563x_2^2 + 0.300x_1x_2 \qquad (36)$$

with an R^2 value of 0.8909. The analysis of variance table is,

Source	df	SS	MS	F
Regression	5	1.6712	0.3342	6.53
Residual	4	0.2048	0.0512	
Total	9	1.8760		

Using the 2 replicate observations at the center of the design to obtain an estimate of the error variance, $s^2 = 0.005$ with 1 degree of freedom, the lack of fit test produced an F value of $F = (0.1998/3)/0.005 = 13.32$, which is not significant at the 0.05 level.

Whether the second-degree coefficients b_{11}, b_{22}, and b_{12} are really necessary may now be tested. This is done by fitting the first-degree model to the 10 thickness values in Table 6 and calculating the regression sum of squares for it. The contribution by the second-degree coefficient estimates to the regression sum of squares for the second-degree model is calculated by taking the difference

SS (2nd-degree terms) = Regression SS (2nd-degree model) − Regression SS (1st-degree model)

The significance of the contribution by the second-degree coefficient estimates is tested using the F test

$$F = \frac{\text{SS (2}^{\text{nd}}\text{-Degree Terms)/No. of Terms (=3)}}{\text{Residual Mean Square with 2nd-Degree Model}} \tag{37}$$

and comparing the value of F with the tabled value of $F_{(3,4,\alpha)}$.

For this example, the first-degree fitted model is

$$\hat{Y} = 7.620 + 0.0396x_1 + 0.1884x_2$$

and the regression SS (1st-degree model) = 0.2965. With the fitted second-degree model (36), regression SS = 1.6712 so that the difference between the regression sum of squares associated with the two models is $1.6712 - 0.2965 = 1.3747$. Thus the value of F in (37) is calculated to be

$$F = \frac{1.3747/3}{0.0512} = 8.95 > F_{(3,4,.05)} = 6.59$$

implying the second-degree coefficient estimates (considered as a group) are significant at the 0.05 level and the decision is taken that the second-degree model (36) is required to represent the disk thickness surface over the experimental region.

With the decision that the fitted model (36) more closely represents the disk thickness surface, than the first-degree model does, it can be used in the search for the highest value of $\hat{Y}$ and the coordinate settings (x_1, x_2) that produce the optimal value of $\hat{Y}$. This search can be done using (i) *graphical methods* and/or (ii) *analytical methods*. The graphical method involves the mapping of the second-order system with a contour plot as in Figure 2. The analytical approach involves taking the derivatives of the estimated second-degree response surface (36) with respect to each x_i, $i = 1, 2, \ldots, k$, setting the derivatives equal to zero, and solving the k equations simultaneously for the values of the x_is. This latter approach of determining the location where the slopes of the response surface (in the directions of the x_i axes) are zero is known as locating the *coordinates of the stationary point*. Both methods will be discussed now.

2.7.1 Graphical Methods: Mapping the Second-Order Surface

The fitted second-degree model (36) can be used to generate a system of contours of the estimated surface by setting $\hat{Y}$ equal to some constant value and mapping the resulting conic in the coordinate system of x_1 and x_2. The contour plot for this example is illustrated in Figure 6b.

The plotted contours suggest that the response surface inside the experimental region is a hill. The nearly circular nature of the contours within the experimental region of the coded variables, x_1 and x_2, results from having forced the experimental region to be a circle of radius $\sqrt{2}$ when defining the design point settings in Table 6 and the approximately equal values, -0.4313 and -0.3563 for b_{11} and b_{22}, respectively. In the system of the original factor levels, X_1 and X_2, the contours would be ellipses.

Using the contour plot of the surface in the region of the coded variables, x_1 and x_2, the coordinate settings of x_1 and x_2 corresponding to the location of the highest estimated disk thickness value are obtained by finding the center of the smallest circle (ellipse) and extrapolating back to the respective axes. These settings are approximately $x_1 = 0.16$ and $x_2 = 0.33$ which correspond to the settings of the original factors of $X_1 = 0.87$ and $X_2 = 0.83$. The estimated highest disk thickness value is found by substituting the values $x_1 = 0.16$ and $x_2 = 0.33$ into Equation 36. This value is $\hat{Y} = 8.32$.

The application of the graphical method for studying the shape of the response surface and determining the approximate location of the highest response value requires the use of a contour plotting program. A second approach that can be used to locate the coordinates of the point where the slope of the surface is zero, and which does not use contour plots, is an analytical approach.

2.7.2 Analytical Method: Locating the Coordinates of the Stationary Point of the Second-Order Surface

The *stationary point* of the response surface is the point where the slopes of the surface, taken in the directions of the x_i axes, $i = 1, 2, \ldots, k$, are zero. The coordinate setting $(x_1, x_2, \ldots, x_k)$ of the stationary point is found by taking the partial derivative of $\hat{Y}$ in (35) with respect to each x_i, setting the derivatives equal to zero, and then simultaneously solving the k equations for the values of x.

Recall the form (36) of the second-order surface for the disk thickness example, which in $k = 2$ variables, is

$$
\begin{aligned}
\hat{Y} &= b_0 + b_1x_1 + b_2x_2 + b_{11}x_1^2 + b_{22}x_2^2 + b_{12}x_1x_2 \\
&= 8.25 + 0.0396x_1 + 0.1884x_2 - 0.4313x_1^2 - 0.3563x_2^2 + 0.300x_1x_2.
\end{aligned} \tag{38}
$$

Taking the partial derivatives of $\hat{Y}$ with respect to x_1 and x_2 and setting them equal to zero yields

$$
\frac{\partial \hat{Y}}{\partial x_1} = b_1 + 2b_{11}x_1 + b_{12}x_2 = 0.0396 - 0.8626x_1 + 0.300x_2 = 0
$$

$$
\tag{39}
$$

$$
\frac{\partial \hat{Y}}{\partial x_2} = b_2 + 2b_{22}x_2 + b_{12}x_1 = 0.1884 - 0.7126x_2 + 0.300x_1 = 0.
$$

The solution (values of x_1 and x_2) to Equation 39 is

$$
x_{01} = \frac{1}{D}(b_2b_{12} - 2b_1b_{22})
$$

$$
x_{02} = \frac{1}{D}(b_1b_{12} - 2b_2b_{11}), \text{ where } D = 4b_{11}b_{22} - b_{12}^2
$$

so that for this example, the following is obtained

$$
x_{01} = \frac{1}{D}[(0.1884)(0.300) - 2(0.0396)(-0.3563)] = 0.1615
$$

$$
\tag{40}
$$

$$
x_{02} = \frac{1}{D}[(0.0396)(0.300) - 2(0.1884)(-0.4313)] = 0.3324
$$

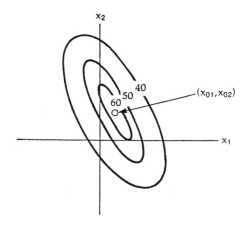

Figure 7a
The stationary point is a maximum

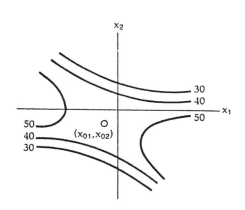

Figure 7b
The stationary point is a minimax point

since $D = 4(-0.4313)(-0.3563) - (0.300)^2 = 0.5246887$. The corresponding settings for the levels of the original factors, using (31), are $X_1 = 0.86$ (ratio of filler/resin) and $X_2 = 0.83$ (position in mold from reference point in cm), respectively.

The estimate of the response at the stationary point is obtained by substituting the values of x_{01} and x_{02} into the fitted model (38) or by using the simpler equation

$$\hat{Y}_0 = b_0 + \tfrac{1}{2}(b_1 x_{01} + b_2 x_{02}). \tag{41}$$

For the values of x_{01} and x_{02} in (40), the estimate is $\hat{Y}_0 = 8.319$. Apart from experimental error in the Y_us, the estimate $\hat{Y}_0 = 8.319$ exceeds all of the observations (the closest exception being $Y_u = 8.3$ at the center of the design). Without the benefit of the contour plot, one would feel confident in assuming that one has located a maximum point of the response surface. In Figure 7a and 7b the stationary points of two surfaces are illustrated where in 7a, the point is a maximum, and in 7b, the point is a minimax (also called saddle point).

2.8 Description of the Surface in the Neighborhood of the Stationary Point

Within the boundaries of the experimental region the contour plot of the disk thickness surface, shown in Figure 6b, described the surface as a hill. When $k = 2$, then the use of a contour plot is all that is needed to obtain an idea of the shape of the response surface in the vicinity of the stationary point (assuming the stationary point is inside the experimental region).

When the number of experimental factors is greater than two ($k > 2$), contour plots of the surface drawn in the plane of the coordinates of two factors, at fixed levels of the remaining $(k - 2)$ factors, can be extremely awkward to use for describing the shape of the response surface in the neighborhood of the stationary point. For higher dimensional $(k > 2)$ problems as well as when discovering, using (40) for $k = 2$, that the location of the stationary point is outside of the experimental region, analytical methods are required for describing the nature of the surface in the vicinity of the stationary point. These methods can be found in textbooks by Davies (1960) Chapter 11, Khuri and Cornell (1987) Chapter 5, Myers (1971) Chapter 5, and Montgomery (1976) chapter 14, and are described briefly now.

In Figure 6 the contours of the disk thickness surface were elliptical in shape and became concentric circles only because the estimate of the pure quadratic terms ($b_{11} = -0.4313$ and $b_{22} = -0.3563$) were approximately equal in value in the fitted model of Equation 36. If the magnitudes of the estimates b_{11} and b_{22} had been quite different, say for example, $b_{11} = 2b_{22}$, then the contours of the surface in the region of the coded variables, x_1 and x_2, would be concentric ellipses with the major and minor axes of the ellipses pointing in directions similar to the x_2 and x_1 axes, respectively. Actually, only if the estimate, b_{12} ($= 0.300$), is zero would the major and minor axes of the ellipses be parallel to the x_2 and x_1 axes, respectively.

As an alternative to expressing the shape of the response surface in terms of the coded variables x_1 and x_2 using the model (36), the response surface can be described in model form using a new set of variables, W_1 and W_2, whose axes represent the principal axes of the response surface and which intersect at the stationary point [i.e., the origin $(W_1, W_2) = (0, 0)$ of the W_1, W_2 system is at (x_{01}, x_{02})], as shown in Figure 8. For example, with the disk thickness surface of Figure 6, it might be preferable to represent the shape of the surface with a second-degree equation in the variables W_1 and W_2 because such an equation can be written in simpler form than the fitted model (36) in x_1 and x_2. This equation is

$$\hat{Y} = \hat{Y}_0 + \lambda_1 W_1^2 + \lambda_2 W_2^2 \tag{42}$$

and is called the *canonical form or equation of the second-degree response surface*. The quantity, $\hat{Y}_0$, is the estimate of the response at the stationary point, $(W_1, W_2) = (0, 0)$, and the coefficients λ_1 and λ_2, are measures of the rate of change of the estimated surface taken along the W_1 and W_2 axes. The values of the coefficients, λ_1 and λ_2, are the values of the characteristic roots (or eigenvalues) of the real symmetric matrix

$$\begin{bmatrix} b_{11} & b_{12}/2 \\ b_{12}/2 & b_{22} \end{bmatrix}$$

where the elements b_{11}, b_{22}, and $b_{12}/2$, of the matrix are measures of curvilinearity as well as interaction between x_1 and x_2 of the estimated surface taken from the model representation (38) of the surface. In (42), the variables W_1 and W_2 are linear functions of x_1 and x_2. For our example, the canonical form (42) is

$$\hat{Y} = 8.319 - 0.239 W_1^2 - 0.548 W_2^2.$$

In general, to express the variables W_1 and W_2 in terms of the variables x_1 and x_2 requires the use of matrix algebra. Since the use of matrices is beyond the scope of this booklet (the exception being the development of least squares in appendix A), the transformation will not be discussed, using matrices, in going from the x-system to the W-system. Rather, the reader is referred to the books by Box and

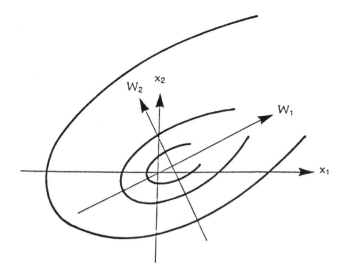

Figure 8
The principal axes of the response surface in the variables W_1 and W_2

Draper (1987), Davies (1960), Khuri and Cornell (1987), Montgomery (1976), and Myers (1971), for a more detailed description of how to derive the canonical equation of a second-degree response surface. The complete canonical analysis of a fitted second-degree response surface is possible by using PROC RSREG of the Statistical Analysis System (SAS, 1982).

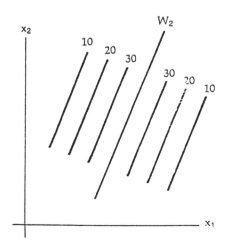

Figure 9a
A stationary ridge

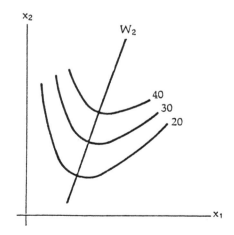

Figure 9b
A rising ridge

2.9 Further Comments on Typical Surfaces Generated by Second-Degree Equations

The nature of typical surfaces generated by a second-degree equation (11) or (35) can be appreciated by its canonical form (42). For two factors, when both coefficients λ_1 and λ_2 are negative, the contours of the fitted surface are ellipses and the surface is a hill. Figure 7a illustrates the case where if the major axis of the elliptical contours points in the same direction as the W_2 axis in Figure 8 then λ_2 is smaller in absolute value than λ_1. When both λ_1 and λ_2 are positive, the surface will be a bowl or basin. When λ_1 and λ_2 are of opposite signs, the contours are hyperbolas as shown in Figure 7b and the surface is saddle-shaped. When λ_1 is negative and λ_2 is zero, the contours are straight lines as in Figure 9a. This may be considered as a limiting situation of either of the above cases (λ_1 and λ_2 have like signs, or λ_1 and λ_2 have opposite signs) and the surface is called a *stationary ridge*. When λ_1 is negative and λ_2 is almost zero and also the location of the stationary point is far outside the experimental region, the contours are parabolas as shown in Figure 9b and the surface is a rising ridge. Again, this may be the limiting case of the ellipses or hyperbolas just mentioned with the stationary point located far away.

With three factors, the contour surfaces can be built up from contour surfaces of two dimensions by superposition. The contour surfaces are again revealed by the signs of λ_1, λ_2, and λ_3. For example, if the signs are (-, -, -), the contour surfaces are ellipsoids. Some typical contour surfaces generated by quadratic equations in three variables are shown in Figure 10.

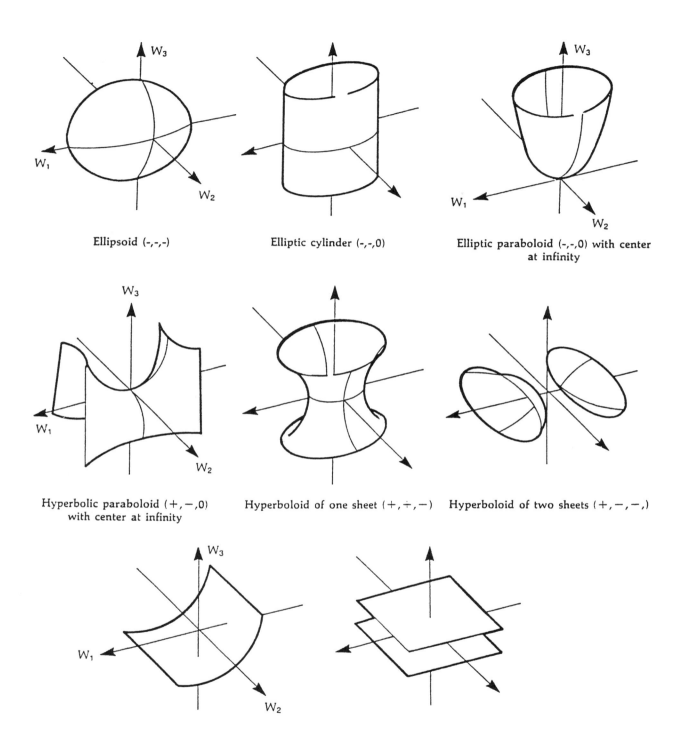

Figure 10
Some higher-dimensional response surfaces, $k = 3$ and signs of $(\lambda_1, \lambda_2, \lambda_3)$

Ellipsoid (-,-,-)

Elliptic cylinder (-,-,0)

Elliptic paraboloid (-,-,0) with center at infinity

Hyperbolic paraboloid (+,−,0) with center at infinity

Hyperboloid of one sheet (+,÷,−)

Hyperboloid of two sheets (+,−,−,)

3

In Section 2.2 two reasons were given for fitting the first-degree polynomial

$$Y = \beta_0 + \beta_1 x_1 + \beta_2 x_2 + \cdots + \beta_k x_k + \epsilon \qquad (43)$$

namely; when the interest is limited only to a *small region* of the factor space and it is assumed the response surface can be approximated reasonably well by the *hyperplane (43)*, or, when it is desirable to obtain a *first approximation of the surface* and the simplest form of the model is fitted initially to assure that the time and cost of experimentation are held to a minimum. A third use for the first-degree fitted model was shown in the steepest ascent procedure where experimentation was performed sequentially in an attempt to *locate higher values of the response*. Still another reason for fitting a first-degree model is when the experimenter is *screening for the most important factors*.

This section will concern itself with designs used for fitting a first-degree model. A *design* is a set of combinations of the levels of the k coded variables which specifies the settings of the levels of the k controllable factors to be performed during the experimentation. With $k = 2$ for example, we saw in Table 1 of the Section 2.3 with the plastic disk manufacturing example that a 2^2 factorial arrangement in x_1 and x_2 fixed the combinations of the settings of filler/resin (ξ_1) and position in the mold (ξ_2) to be $(X_1, X_2) = (5/8, 1.5), (5/8, 2.5), (7/8, 1.5),$ and $(7/8, 2.5)$. Geometrically, the locations of the four design points represent the coordinates of the vertices of a square which is centered at $(X_1, X_2) = (6/8, 2)$, which in the design variables is at $(x_1, x_2) = (0, 0)$. Later in Table 6, the coordinates of x_1 and x_2 were shown to be eight points equispaced on the perimeter of a circle of radius $\sqrt{2}$ plus a point at the center of the circle; see Figure 6b. Such a design was not selected arbitrarily but rather because it possessed desirable properties. Fourteen such design properties are listed by Box and Draper (1975), some of which are: the design should

i. generate a satisfactory distribution of information throughout the region of interest,

ii. ensure that the fitted model predicts a value, $\hat{Y}$, at all points in the region of interest that is as close as possible to the true value of the response,

iii. give good detectability of model lack of fit,

iv. allow experiments to be performed in blocks,

v. allow designs of increasing order to be built up sequentially,

vi. provide an internal estimate of the error variance, and

vii. ensure simplicity of calculation of the coefficient estimates.

Most of the design criteria for choosing one response surface design over another, center around the properties (the variance and bias) of the fitted model. In particular, if the fitted first-degree model is used to predict a value of the response at some point $(x_1, x_2, \ldots, x_k)$ in the experimental region, *the prediction equation* is written as

$$\hat{Y}(\mathbf{x}) = b_0 + b_1 x_1 + b_2 x_2 + \cdots + b_k x_k \tag{44}$$

where the bs are estimates of the βs in (43) and $\hat{Y}(\mathbf{x})$ is hereafter used to denote the value of $\hat{Y}$ at $\mathbf{x}$. The coordinates of the x's at the point $(x_1, x_2, \ldots, x_k)$ are substituted into Equation 44 to produce the value $\hat{Y}(\mathbf{x})$. Examples of predicted response values, taken at the design settings, are listed in Table 3. These predicted values were used to calculate the residuals, $(Y_u - \hat{Y}_u)$, at the design points while squares of the residuals were summed to produce SSE.

A measure of precision associated with the predicted value, $\hat{Y}(\mathbf{x})$, is the variance $\hat{Y}(\mathbf{x})$, written as

$$\begin{aligned}
\mathrm{Var}[\hat{Y}(\mathbf{x})] &= \mathrm{Var}[b_0 + b_1 x_1 + b_2 x_2 + \cdots + b_k x_k] \\
&= \sum_{i=0}^{k} x_i^2 \, \mathrm{Var}(b_i) + 2 \sum_{\substack{i<j \\ i=0}}^{k} x_i x_j \, \mathrm{Cov}(b_i, b_j), \quad x_0 = 1
\end{aligned} \tag{45}$$

where $\mathrm{Var}(b_i)$ is the variance of b_i $(0 \leq i \leq k)$ and $\mathrm{Cov}(b_i, b_j)$ is the covariance of b_i and b_j $(0 \leq i < j \leq k)$. Since the values of the x's in (45) are fixed to be the coordinate settings of the point $(x_1, x_2, \ldots, x_k)$ at which the prediction is made, then the magnitude of $\mathrm{Var}[\hat{Y}(\mathbf{x})]$ depends on the magnitude of the $\mathrm{Var}(b_i)$ as well as the $\mathrm{Cov}(b_i, b_j)$. In Appendix A, it is shown in Equation A5 that the variance-covariance matrix of the coefficient estimates is written as $(\mathbf{X}'\mathbf{X})^{-1} \sigma^2$ where in the matrix $\mathbf{X}$ the design settings of the coded variables $x_1, x_2, \ldots, x_k$ are contained. Thus, the magnitudes of the $\mathrm{Var}(b_i)$ and the $\mathrm{Cov}(b_i, b_j)$ are affected by the design settings in $x_1, x_2, \ldots, x_k$ as is the magnitude of $\mathrm{Var}[\hat{Y}(\mathbf{x})]$ in (45).

In the remainder of this section, the following notation will be used. Write the *coordinates* of n distinct design points in k-variable space in array form as

design point					
1	x_{11}	x_{12}	x_{13}	$\cdots$	x_{1k}
2	x_{21}	x_{22}	x_{23}	$\cdots$	x_{2k}
3	x_{31}	x_{32}	x_{33}	$\cdots$	x_{3k}
$\vdots$	$\vdots$	$\vdots$	$\vdots$		$\vdots$
n	x_{n1}	x_{n2}	x_{n3}	$\cdots$	x_{nk}

$$\tag{46}$$

where in the uth row $(1 \leq u \leq n)$, the values of $x_{u1}, x_{u2}, x_{u3}, \ldots, x_{uk}$ represent the coordinate settings of $x_1, x_2, x_3, \ldots, x_k$ at the uth design point. The array in

(46) shall be referred to as the *design array*. For example, in Table 2, the *design array* for x_1 and x_2 consisted of the 4 rows of elements

$$
\begin{array}{cc}
-1 & -1 \\
-1 & +1 \\
+1 & -1 \\
+1 & +1
\end{array}
$$

while the *design array* in Table 6 consisted of the top 9 rows

$$
\begin{array}{cc}
-1 & -1 \\
1 & 1 \\
\vdots & \vdots \\
0 & \sqrt{2} \\
0 & 0 \\
0 & 0.
\end{array}
$$

The 10th row is a duplication of the 9th row and indicates a second replicated observation was collected at the center of the (x_1, x_2)-region. Since the elements, the $x_{ui}s$, of the design array are values of the coded variables, the sums of the values in each column of the design array are required to be equal to zero, i.e., $\Sigma_{u=1}^{n} x_{ui} = 0$. If replicate observations are collected at one or more design points, the replicates are taken usually at the center of the design or an equal number of replicates is collected at each design point so that $\Sigma_{u=1}^{N} x_{ui} = 0$ where N is the total number of observations $(N \geq n)$.

Definition 1: A first-order *orthogonal* design is a design for which the columns of the design array are orthogonal, that is,

$$
\sum_{u=1}^{n} x_{ui}x_{uj} = 0 \text{ for all } i, j = 1, 2, \ldots, k, i \neq j. \tag{47}
$$

Furthermore, if replicate observations are collected at some of the design points (i.e., some rows of the array are repeated) so that the total number, N, of observations exceeds n, then for an orthogonal design

$$
\sum_{u=1}^{N} x_{ui}x_{uj} = 0 \text{ for all } i, j = 1, 2, \ldots, k, i \neq j. \tag{48}
$$

Orthogonal first-order designs are *optimal* in the sense of providing *minimum variance* estimates of the coefficients in (43). Furthermore, with orthogonal first-order designs, the $\text{Cov}(b_i, b_j)$ quantities in (45) are all zero so that

$$
\text{Var}[\hat{Y}(\mathbf{x})] = \text{Var}(b_0) + \sum_{i=1}^{k} x_i^2 \text{Var}(b_i). \tag{49}
$$

With a first-order orthogonal design, the estimates b_0 and b_i of the β_0 and β_i coefficients are uncorrelated.

In the remainder of this Section 3 the discussion of first-order designs will be restricted to the class of orthogonal designs. In particular, the following will be discussed

a. 2^k factorial arrangements
b. some fractional 2^k factorial arrangements (i.e., 2^{k-1} and 2^{k-2} factorials)
c. simplex designs
d. Plackett-Burman designs

3.1 The 2^k Factorial Arrangements

In the 2^k factorial arrangement, each factor (ξ_i) is measured at two levels only ($X_{i\text{LOW}}$ and $X_{i\text{HIGH}}$). These levels are coded as in (9) to produce the values ± 1 for the corresponding coded variable x_i. By considering all possible combinations of the levels of the k factors, a design consisting of 2^k points, which will be called the *2^k factorial arrangement*.

The elements, x_{ui}, of the design array (46) for a 2^k factorial arrangement consists only of ± 1. Thus, for the first-degree fitted model (44), the variances of the estimates $b_0, b_1, \ldots, b_k$ are, as shown in (14), equal to $\text{Var}(b_i) = \sigma^2/N$, $0 \leq i \leq k$. Consequently, from (49), the variance of the predicted response $\hat{Y}$ at the point $(x_1, x_2, \ldots, x_k)$ is

$$\text{Var}[\hat{Y}(\mathbf{x})] = \frac{\sigma^2}{N} + \sum_{i=1}^{k} x_i^2 \frac{\sigma^2}{N}$$

$$= \frac{\sigma^2}{N} (1 + \rho^2)$$

where $\rho = \sqrt{x_1^2 + x_2^2 + \cdots + x_k^2}$ is the distance from the center of the design to the point $(x_1, x_2, \ldots, x_k)$. In other words, the magnitude of the $\text{Var}[\hat{Y}(\mathbf{x})]$ is a function of σ^2, the variance of the errors in the model (43), the total number, N, of observations, and ρ^2, the square of the distance from the center of the design to the point $(x_1, x_2, \ldots, x_k)$. If σ^2 is known and N is held fixed, then $\text{Var}[\hat{Y}(\mathbf{x})]$ depends only on the distance the point $(x_1, x_2, \ldots, x_k)$ lies from the center of the design and does not depend on the direction that the point $(x_1, x_2, \ldots, x_k)$ is positioned relative to the x_i-axes. This property of the variance of $\hat{Y}(\mathbf{x})$ implies the class of 2^k factorials belong to a larger class of designs called *rotatable designs*.

3.1.1 Rotatable Designs

Definition 2: A design is said to be *rotatable* if upon rotating the points of the design about the center $(x_1, x_2, \ldots, x_k) = (0, 0, \ldots, 0)$ the moments of the distribution of the design points remain unchanged. For a rotatable design the variance of the predicted response, $\hat{Y}(\mathbf{x})$, is constant at all points that are equidistant from the center of the design. This implies that the variance contours of $\hat{Y}(\mathbf{x})$ are concentric circles in two dimensions and the contours are concentric spheres in three dimensions.

A *first-order rotatable design* is a set of points, equally spaced on a circle ($k = 2$), or a sphere ($k = 3$), or a hypersphere ($k \geq 4$) and thus forming the vertices of a regular polygon in a plane, or polyhedron in three-dimensional space, or polytope in higher-dimensional space. Examples of first-order rotatable designs provided by the vertices of a regular polygon are discussed in Section 4.4.1 since these designs, when augmented with at least one center point, are more frequently used for fitting the second-degree polynomial. As mentioned previously, the 2^k factorial arrangements are also examples of first-order rotatable designs.

In three dimensions ($k = 3$), sets of n points equally spaced on a sphere are provided by the vertices of five regular figures. These are the tetrahedron ($n = 4$), the octahedron ($n = 6$), the cube ($n = 8$), the icosahedron ($n = 12$), and the dodecahedron ($n = 20$). Section 4.4.1 discusses how to construct rotatable designs of second order by combining some of these regular figures.

3.2 Fractions of the 2^k Factorial Arrangements

In many experimental programs, two reasons stand out for choosing not to perform all of the 2^k factor-level combinations of a complete factorial arrangement. Firstly, as the number, k, of factors increases, the number of factor-level combinations rapidly becomes large; e.g., when $k = 7$, $2^7 = 128$. Secondly, with a complete 2^k factorial arrangement, although it is possible to estimate all of the coefficients (2^k in number) in the model

$$Y = \beta_0 + \sum_{i=1}^{k} \beta_i x_i + \sum_{i<j}^{k}\sum \beta_{ij} x_i x_j + \sum_{i<j<l}^{k}\sum\sum \beta_{ijl} x_i x_j x_l + \cdots \qquad (51)$$
$$+ \beta_{12\ldots k} x_1 x_2 \ldots x_k + \epsilon$$

only the first $k + 1$ terms of the model define the equation of a hyperplane. The remaining $2^k - (k + 1)$ terms, consisting of crossproducts among the x_i, x_j, and x_k along with the coefficients β_{ij}, β_{ijk}, . . . , are measures of the distortion of the hyperplane and are due to *interactions* among the factors. Often times the interaction effects either are negligible or are not of interest and a reduction in the number of terms in the model (51) is sought accompanied by a reduction in the number of design points. The reduction in the number of design points is possible by using only a *fractional replicate* of the 2^k factorial arrangement.

A fractional replicate of a 2^k factorial is, as the name implies, a fraction or subset of the 2^k factor-level combinations. A ½ fractional replicate, denoted by 2^{k-1}, contains one-half the number of points of the 2^k arrangement. A ¼ fractional replicate, or 2^{k-2}, contains one-fourth the number of points of the 2^k arrangement. Fractional replicates are required to have properties similar to that of the complete factorial in that they must contain enough points to allow the estimation of the $k + 1$ coefficients in the first-degree model (43) in addition to being orthogonal.

This booklet will not be concerned with the construction of fractional replicates since there are many textbooks that cover this topic in detail; see for example, Box, Hunter, and Hunter (1978) Chapter 12, Montgomery (1976) Chapter 10.

Instead, an example of a 2^{4-1} fractional factorial experiment will be presented and the reader is referred to appendix C for a listing of some fractional design plans.

3.2.1 An Example of a 2^{4-1} Fractional Replicate Experiment

The following example was taken from Box, Hunter, and Hunter (1978), Chapter 10, pp 324–328. A process development study was undertaken to measure the effects of the factors, catalyst charge (X_1), temperature (X_2), pressure (X_3), and concentration (X_4), on the response, conversion (Y). The listing of the factor levels and the recorded percent conversion values for the entire set of $2^4 = 16$ factor-level combinations is given in Table 7. The values of the coded variables are defined as $x_1 = (X_1 - 12.5)/2.5$, $x_2 = (X_2 - 230)/10$, $x_3 = (X_3 - 65)/15$, and $x_4 = (X_4 - 11)/1$.

Suppose that instead of performing the complete set of 16 experiments, the experimenter selects to perform only $2^{4-1} =$ eight experiments for the purpose of estimating the coefficients in the first-degree model

$$Y = \beta_0 + \beta_1 x_1 + \beta_2 x_2 + \beta_3 x_3 + \beta_4 x_4 + \epsilon. \tag{52}$$

The eight chosen experiments have been denoted by marking their recorded conversion values in Table 7 with an asterisk (*). Thus only the data in Table 8 are available to estimate the coefficients in (52).

Table 7
Data Obtained in a Process Development Study

Factors				Coded Variables				
Cat. Charge X_1 (lb)	Temperature X_2 (°C)	Pressure X_3 (psi)	Concentration X_4 (%)	x_1	x_2	x_3	x_4	Conversion (%)
10	220	50	10	−1	−1	−1	−1	71*
15	220	50	10	1	−1	−1	−1	61
10	240	50	10	−1	1	−1	−1	90
15	240	50	10	1	1	−1	−1	82*
10	220	80	10	−1	−1	1	−1	68
15	220	80	10	1	−1	1	−1	61*
10	240	80	10	−1	1	1	−1	87*
15	240	80	10	1	1	1	−1	80
10	220	50	12	−1	−1	−1	1	61
15	220	50	12	1	−1	−1	1	50*
10	240	50	12	−1	1	−1	1	89*
15	240	50	12	1	1	−1	1	83
10	220	80	12	−1	−1	1	1	59*
15	220	80	12	1	−1	1	1	51
10	240	80	12	−1	1	1	1	85
15	240	80	12	1	1	1	1	78*

Table 8
Date for the 2^{4-1} Fractional Replicate and the
Sequence of Performing the Experiments

| Coded Variables | | | | Experimental | Conversion |
x_1	x_2	x_3	x_4	Sequence	(%)
-1	1	1	-1	1	87
1	1	-1	-1	2	82
-1	-1	1	1	3	59
-1	-1	-1	-1	4	71
1	-1	1	-1	5	61
1	1	1	1	6	78
1	-1	-1	1	7	50
-1	1	-1	1	8	89

The estimates of the coefficients using the data from Table 8 and the formulas (13) are

$$
\begin{aligned}
b_0 &= \bar{Y} = 72.125 \\
b_1 &= \tfrac{1}{2}[\bar{Y}_{x_1=1} - \bar{Y}_{x_1=-1}] = \tfrac{1}{2}[67.75 - 76.50] = -4.375 \\
b_2 &= \tfrac{1}{2}[84.00 - 60.25] = 11.875 \\
b_3 &= -0.875, \text{ and } b_4 = -3.125.
\end{aligned}
\tag{53}
$$

The fitted model is

$$
\hat{Y} = 72.125 - 4.375x_1 + 11.875x_2 - 0.875x_3 - 3.125x_4.
\tag{54}
$$

The analysis of variance table is

Source	df		Mean Square	F	
Regression	4	1365.500	341.375	17.25	$> F_{(4,3,0.05)} = 9.12$
Residual	3	59.375	19.792		
Total	7	1424.875			

where the significant F ratio is a test of the null hypothesis $H_0: \beta_1 = \beta_2 = \beta_3 = \beta_4 = 0$ of the coefficients in the model (52).

At this point, two questions naturally are raised. First, what are the *interpretations of the coefficient estimates* in (53)? Secondly, *how were the specific 8 factor level combinations in* Table 8 selected from the entire set of $2^4 = 16$ combinations in Table 7? The first question will be addressed now after which a brief comment on the construction of the fractional replicate plan of Table 8 will be made.

To understand the interpretations of the coefficient estimates in the model (54), it must first be recognized that with the entire set of 16 data values in Table 7, it is possible to estimate 15 separate factorial effects. To be more specific, let the factors catalyst charge, temperature, pressure, and concentration be denoted by A, B, C, and D, respectively. The effects that could be estimated with the 16 data values are

   i. the main effects of each of the factors denoted by A, B, C, and D,
  ii. the six 2-factor interaction effects denoted by AB, AC, AD, BC, BD, and CD,
 iii. the four 3-factor interaction effects ABC, ABD, ACD, and BCD, and
 iv. the 4-factor interaction effect ABCD.

For example, using the 16 data values, the *main effect* of factor A is calculated as

$$\bar{Y}_{15 \text{ lbs}} - \bar{Y}_{10 \text{ lbs}} = 68.25 - 76.25 = -8.00$$

where $\bar{Y}_{15}$ is the average of the eight conversion values at $X_1 = 15$ (or $x_1 = 1$). The main effect of A represents the change in the average conversion value (%) when the catalyst charge is raised from 10 to 15 lb. The *interaction effect* between factors A and B is calculated as

$$\begin{aligned}&\tfrac{1}{2}[(\bar{Y}_{15,240} - \bar{Y}_{10,240}) - (\bar{Y}_{15,220} - \bar{Y}_{10,220})]\\&= \tfrac{1}{2}[(80.75 - 87.75) - (55.75 - 64.75)] = 1.0\end{aligned}$$

where $\bar{Y}_{15,240}$ for example is the average conversion value at the combination of $X_1 = 15$ and $X_2 = 240$ (or at $x_1 = 1$ and $x_2 = 1$). The value of the interaction effect between A and B represents *half the difference* between the effect of catalyst charge at the high temperature level (240°C) and the effect of catalyst charge at the low temperature level (220°C).

The 15 factorial effects listed in (i), (ii), (iii), and (iv) are estimable by fitting the 16 data values in Table 7 using the complete model

$$Y = \gamma_0 + \sum_{i=1}^{4} \gamma_i x_i + \sum_{i<j}^{4} \gamma_{ij} x_i x_j + \sum_{i<j<l}^{4} \gamma_{ijl} x_i x_j x_l + \gamma_{1234} x_1 x_2 x_3 x_4 + \epsilon. \tag{55}$$

In particular, using the values ± 1 to denote the levels for the coded variables x_1, x_2, x_3, and x_4, for some of the coefficient estimates, the values are

$$\begin{aligned}
g_0 &= 72.25 = \text{the average of the 16 response values}\\
g_1 &= -4.00 = \tfrac{1}{2}(\text{main effect of factor A})\\
g_2 &= 12.00 = \tfrac{1}{2}(\text{main effect of factor B})\\
g_{12} &= 0.50 = \tfrac{1}{2}(\text{2-factor interaction effect AB})\\
g_{123} &= -0.375 = \tfrac{1}{2}(\text{3-factor interaction effect ABC})\\
g_{1234} &= -0.125 = \tfrac{1}{2}(\text{4-factor interaction effect ABCD})
\end{aligned} \tag{56}$$

where the g's are estimates of the γ's.

Returning to the first-degree model (54) that was fitted to the eight data values in Table 8, since only half of the total number (16) of observations was used, all 15 factorial effects listed in (i), (ii), (iii), and (iv) cannot be expected to be estimated. In fact, with the model (52) when only the five coefficients, β_0, β_1, β_2, β_3, and β_4 were estimated, in a sense it was accepted that coefficient estimates b_0, b_1, b_2, b_3, and b_4, will be estimates of linear combinations of the γ's in (55). That this is indeed the case can be verified by checking the values of the b's in (53) with the values of the g's in (56) and noticing that

$$
\begin{aligned}
b_0 &= g_0 + g_{1234} \\
b_1 &= g_1 + g_{234} \\
b_2 &= g_2 + g_{134} \\
b_3 &= g_3 + g_{124} \\
b_4 &= g_4 + g_{123}.
\end{aligned}
\tag{57}
$$

Thus, the coefficient β_1 in model (52) is equal to the sum of the coefficients γ_1 and γ_{234} in model (55) and the factorial effects that are represented by the coefficients γ_1 and γ_{234} are said to be *aliases* of each other when using the ½ fractional design of Table 8. Factorial effects that are aliased with each other cannot be measured separately and are said to be *confounded*.

A brief comment will be made on the choice of the specific factor-level combinations of the coded variables that were marked with an asterisk in Table 7 and made up the 2^{4-1} fractional replicate arrangement in Table 8. The first three columns (the x_1, x_2, and x_3 columns) of Table 8 comprise a complete 2^3 factorial arrangement. Now, with the variables x_1, x_2, and x_3, suppose columns of ± 1 values in Table 8 were constructed corresponding to the crossproducts $x_1 x_2$, $x_1 x_3$, $x_2 x_3$, and $x_1 x_2 x_3$. Now, in Table 8, the element in each row of the x_4 column corresponds exactly to the element in each row of the $x_1 x_2 x_3$ column from which $x_4 = x_1 x_2 x_3$ is inferred. This relationship, $x_4 = x_1 x_2 x_3$, is called the *generator* of the design (see Box, Hunter, and Hunter (1978), p.383) and can also be written as $I = x_1 x_2 x_3 x_4$. It is interesting to note that three other 2^{4-1} fractional replicate arrangements could have been generated by setting $x_4 = x_1 x_2$, $x_4 = x_2 x_3$, and $x_4 = x_1 x_3$. The first two plans are listed in appendix C.

Two final remarks on the use of a ½ fractional replicate design when fitting a first-degree model of the form (43) are worth mentioning. First, no measure of the possible lack of fit of the model is provided unless one has an estimate of the error variance from previous experimentation or one chooses to obtain an estimate of the error variance by performing some center point replications. Secondly, if an $x_i x_j x_l$ interaction term in the model (55) really exists, it will bias the estimate of the main effect associated with x_k, i.e., if γ_{123} exists it will bias the estimation of β_4. In most industrial experiments, however, it is rare to discover that three- and higher-factor interactions are present and therefore the use of fractional factorials is recommended when fitting first-order models and the number of factors is large, i.e., for $k \geq 5$.

3.3 Simplex Designs

The *simplex design* is an orthogonal design consisting of $n = k + 1$ points where k is the number of variables in the first-degree model. The design points are located at the vertices of a k-dimensional regular-sided figure (or simplex) and are characterized by the property that the angle, θ, that any two points make with the origin is such that $\cos \theta = -1/k$. For $k = 2$, the design points form the vertices of an equilateral triangle, and for $k = 3$, the design points form the vertices of a tetrahedron as shown in Figures 11a and 11b, respectively.

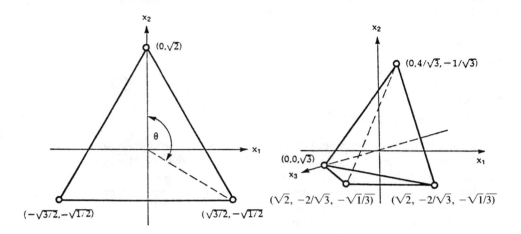

Figure 11a
Simplex design for $k = 2$

Figure 11b
Simplex design for $k = 3$

The *design array* (46) for a simplex design in k variables can be written in the general form as

$$
\begin{array}{ccccc}
x_1 & x_2 & x_3 & \cdots & x_k \\
\hline
-s_1 & -s_2 & -s_3 & \cdots & -s_k \\
s_1 & -s_2 & -s_3 & \cdots & -s_k \\
0 & 2s_2 & -s_3 & \cdots & -s_k \\
0 & 0 & 3s_3 & \cdots & -s_k \\
0 & 0 & 0 & \cdots & -s_k \\
\vdots & \vdots & \vdots & & \vdots \\
0 & 0 & 0 & \cdots & ks_k
\end{array}
\tag{58}
$$

where $s_i = \{c(k + 1)/[i(i + 1)]\}^{1/2}$ and c is a constant to be selected. For example, if it is required that the sum of squares of the elements in each column be unity, then $c = 1/(k + 1)$. If the sum of squares is to equal N, as is usually the case, then $c = 1$. Also, the columns of the design array (58) can be interchanged, which amounts to rotating the design points about the center of the design, without affecting the variance of the estimates of the coefficients in the first degree model. Thus, since the simplex design is an orthogonal design, and from (49),

$$
\text{Var}[\hat{Y}(\mathbf{x})] = \text{Var}(b_0) + \sum_{i=1}^{k} x_i^2 \, \text{Var}\,(b_i)
$$

then the value of the $\text{Var}[\hat{Y}(\mathbf{x})]$ is unaffected also by a rotation of the design points, which means the simplex designs are also rotatable designs. The design arrays for two simplex designs for $k = 2$ and where $c = 1$ are shown below. The locations of the points 1, 2, and 3 of design 2 are the result of rotating (counter clockwise) the points 1, 3, and 2 of design 1 through an angle of 30°.

Point	Design 1 x_1	x_2	Design 2 x_1	x_2
1	$-\sqrt{3/2}$	$-1/\sqrt{2}$	$-1/\sqrt{2}$	$-\sqrt{3/2}$
2	$\sqrt{3/2}$	$-1/\sqrt{2}$	$-1/\sqrt{2}$	$\sqrt{3/2}$
3	0	$\sqrt{2}$	$\sqrt{2}$	0

With designs 1 and 2, the value of the $\text{Var}[\hat{Y}(\mathbf{x})]$ at the point $\mathbf{x} = (x_1, x_2)$ is

$$\text{Var}[\hat{Y}(\mathbf{x})] = \frac{1}{3}(1 + x_1^2 + x_2^2)\sigma^2$$

where σ^2 is the variance of a single observation.

Since the number of design points in the simplex design is equal to the number of coefficients in the model to be estimated, the addition of center point replicates is often recommended so that an estimate of the error variance could be obtained or a test for curvature could be performed. Such a test was described in Section 2.6.2.

3.4 Plackett-Burman Designs

These designs are fractions of the 2^k factorial arrangements. The number of design points is $n = k + 1$ where n is a multiple of 4. With a Plackett-Burman design, the coefficients in the first-degree model are estimated with maximum precision (on a per point basis).

To construct a Plackett-Burman design for fitting a first-degree model in k variables, first select a row of the design array (46) consisting of $(k + 1)/2$ $+1s$ and $(k - 1)/2$ $-1s$ and designate this row as the top row in the newly constructed design array. The next $k - 1$ rows of the new array are generated from the first row by shifting them each cyclically one place to the right. Finally, the last row of the new array is a row of $-1s$. The new array contains $n = k + 1$ rows.

To illustrate, let $k = 7$ so that $n = 7 + 1 = 8$ is a multiple of 4. Choosing from the design array of a 2^7 factorial, the following row of values for the coded variables, consisting of $(7 + 1)/2 = 4$ $+1s$ and $(7 - 1)/2 = 3$ $-1s$ which was generated using $I = x_1 x_2 x_3 x_5$,

x_1	x_2	x_3	x_4	x_5	x_6	x_7
+1	+1	+1	−1	+1	−1	−1

The next six rows are

$$
\begin{array}{rrrrrrr}
-1 & +1 & +1 & +1 & -1 & +1 & -1 \\
-1 & -1 & +1 & +1 & +1 & -1 & +1 \\
+1 & -1 & -1 & +1 & +1 & +1 & -1 \\
-1 & +1 & -1 & -1 & +1 & +1 & +1 \\
+1 & -1 & +1 & -1 & -1 & +1 & +1 \\
+1 & +1 & -1 & +1 & -1 & -1 & +1 \\
\end{array}
$$

and the last row is

$$
\begin{array}{rrrrrrr}
-1 & -1 & -1 & -1 & -1 & -1 & -1.
\end{array}
$$

These eight rows comprise a design array that can be used to fit the first-degree model

$$
Y = \beta_0 + \beta_1 x_1 + \beta_2 x_2 + \beta_3 x_3 + \beta_4 x_4 + \beta_5 x_5 + \beta_6 x_6 + \beta_7 x_7 + \epsilon.
$$

The selection of the top row, from which the rest of the design is generated, is discussed in Plackett and Burman (1946).

4

In Section 2.7, the second-degree model (34), where $k = 2$, was fitted to ten disk thickness values resulting in the fitted model (36). The disks were manufactured according to nine different combinations of filler/resin and position in the mold. The specific combinations of x_1 and x_2 were defined using the points of a central-composite design whose design coordinates are listed in Table 6 and are displayed in Figure 6b. In Section 3.0, the central composite design was chosen for this example because it possessed desirable properties. Such properties are described in more detail in Section 4.2.

4.0 Designs for Fitting Second-Degree Models

One of the first class of designs that comes to mind for collecting observations in which to estimate the coefficients in the second-degree model

$$Y = \beta_0 + \sum_{i=1}^{k} \beta_i x_i + \sum_{i=1}^{k} \beta_{ii} x_i^2 + \sum \sum_{i<j}^{k} \beta_{ij} x_i x_j + \epsilon \qquad (59)$$

4.1 The 3^k Factorial Arrangements

is the *3^k factorial arrangement*. In the 3^k factorial, each factor (ξ_i) has three levels, which when equally spaced, produces the coded values $x_i = -1, 0, +1$ using once again the coding formula (9). The total number of factor level combinations (design points) is $n = 3^k$, which can be excessively large. To reduce the total number of design points, a 3^{k-m} fractional replicate design could be used $(m < k)$. A general procedure for constructing 3^{k-m} fractional replicates is given in Montgomery (1976), Chapter 10. Tables of 3^{k-m} fractional design plans are provided in Connor and Zelen (1959).

4.2 The Central Composite Design

Perhaps the most popular class of designs used for estimating the coefficients in the second-degree model (59) is the class of *composite designs* of which the *central composite design* (abbreviated ccd) is a member. These designs (the ccd) consist of

i. the 2^k vertices of a k-dimensional "cube" (or a suitable 2^{k-m} fractional replicate when $k \geq 5$), where the factor levels are coded as in (9) so that the design center is at $(0, 0, \ldots, 0)$. The values of the coded variables in this factorial portion of the design are $(x_1, x_2, \ldots, x_k) = (\pm 1, \pm 1, \ldots, \pm 1)$,

ii. the $2k$ vertices $(\pm \alpha, 0, 0, \ldots, 0), (0, \pm \alpha, 0, \ldots, 0), \ldots, (0, 0, \ldots, 0, \pm \alpha)$ of a k-dimensional "octahedron" or "star," and

iii. $n_0 \geq 1$ center point replicates $(x_1, x_2, \ldots, x_k) = (0, 0, \ldots, 0)$.

The total number of distinct design points is $n = 2^k + 2k + n_0$ or $n = 2^{k-m} + 2k + n_0$ when a fractional replicate is used in (i). The choice of the number, n_0, of center point replicates and of the value of α in (ii) will be explained shortly. In Figures 12a and 12b are drawn ccds for $k = 2$ and $k = 3$ variables, respectively.

The ccd may possess the constant $\text{Var}[\hat{Y}(\mathbf{x})]$ property of a rotatable design (see Section 3.1.1) or the ccd may be an orthogonal design, in which case the individual effects of the k variables can be assessed independently. However, to obtain the property of orthogonality, the terms in the model (59) have to be redefined in terms of orthogonal polynomials as discussed in Box and Hunter (1957) and Khuri and Cornell (1987), Chapter 4. The reparameterization of the second-degree model to achieve orthogonality will not be discussed; instead, concentration will be on the rotatability property since this is related to the precision of the predicted value, $\hat{Y}(\mathbf{x})$, which is important. The rotatability property is achieved by selecting appropriate values for n_0 and α in (iii) and (ii) above.

For the ccd to be rotatable, n_0 can be any integer greater than zero but the value of α in (ii) must be equal to

$$\alpha = \sqrt[4]{M} \tag{60}$$

where M is the number of factorial points in (i), that is, $M = 2^k$ or $M = 2^{k-m}$. If r

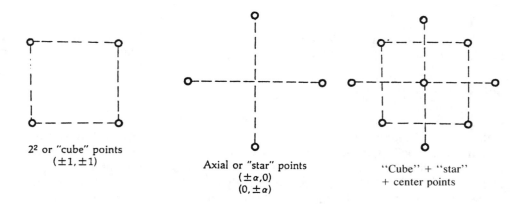

2² or "cube" points
$(\pm 1, \pm 1)$

Axial or "star" points
$(\pm \alpha, 0)$
$(0, \pm \alpha)$

"Cube" + "star"
+ center points

Figure 12a
CCD for $k = 2$ variables

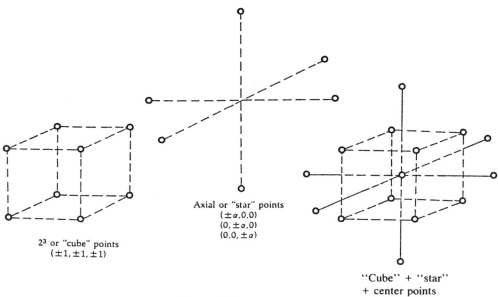

Figure 12b
CCD for k = 3 variables

2³ or "cube" points
($\pm 1, \pm 1, \pm 1$)

Axial or "star" points
($\pm a$,0,0)
(0,$\pm a$,0)
(0,0,$\pm a$)

"Cube" + "star"
+ center points

replicate observations are collected at each point of the 2^k factorial, then $M = r2^k$. Table 9 lists the coordinate values of the coded variables for a ccd for $k = 2$ and $k = 3$, respectively, with $n_0 = 1$, while Table 10 lists values for α for the design to be rotatable for $k = 2, 3, 4, 5, 6$, and 7 variables.

Table 9
Central Composite Design Settings

$k = 2$		$k = 3$		
x_1	x_2	x_1	x_2	x_3
−1	−1	−1	−1	−1
1	−1	1	−1	−1
−1	1	−1	1	−1
1	1	1	1	−1
$-\sqrt{2}$	0	−1	−1	1
$\sqrt{2}$	0	1	−1	1
0	$-\sqrt{2}$	−1	1	1
0	$\sqrt{2}$	1	1	1
0	0	−1.682	0	0
		1.682	0	0
		0	−1.682	0
		0	1.682	0
		0	0	−1.682
		0	0	1.682
		0	0	0

Table 10
Values of α for the CCD to Be Rotatable

$k =$	2	3	4	5	6	6(½ rep)	7	7(½ rep)
$p = (k + 1)(k + 2)/2$	6	10	15	21	28		36	
$M + 2k$	8	14	24	42	76	44	142	78
α (rot)	1.414	1.682	2.000	2.378	2.828	2.378	3.364	2.828

4.3 Orthogonal Blocking of the CCD

In the list in Section 3.0 of desirable properties of a response surface design, property (iv) stated the design should allow experiments to be performed *in blocks*. Some examples of blocks in an industrial environment might be the different shifts of plant personnel, different batches of raw material from the same vendor, or different vendors supplying the raw material or separate laboratories performing the experiments. These changing experimental conditions are most likely to occur whenever the total number of experiments is large or when the investigation of the response system is conducted using a sequence of smaller groups of experiments such as:

i. the fitting of a first-degree model to the points of a first-order design. This initial group of experiments is also used to test the adequacy of the fitted model and if the model is found to be inadequate (perhaps due to curvature in the surface say), and

ii. a second group (and possibly a third group) of experiments is performed to enable the fitting of a second-degree model. The design points used for fitting the second-degree model would be the points defined for the second group or block of experiments plus the points used in fitting the first-degree model in (i).

If the block effects (or different environmental conditions) can be estimated separately and independently from the factors (ξ_1, ξ_2, . . . , ξ_k) affecting the response, or stated another way, if the block effects will in no manner affect the estimates of the first- and second-order coefficients in the second-degree model, then the design is said to *block orthogonally*.

The ccd is a design that allows orthogonal blocking. When two or more blocks are to be considered, the choice of the value of the axial settings, α, and the number of center point replicates, n_0, must be taken into account to achieve the orthogonal blocking property. First, however, two conditions of the design must be satisfied.

1. Each block must contain a first-order orthogonal design. That is to say, in each block the columns of the design array (46) must satisfy (47) and (48).

2. The fraction of the total sum of squares of each variable x_i in each (and every) block must be equal to the fraction of the total number of observations allotted to that block. In other words, for the lth block, $l = 1, 2, . . . , b$

$$\frac{\sum_{u=1}^{n_l} x_{ui}^2}{\sum_{u=1}^{N} x_{ui}^2} = \frac{n_l}{N} \tag{61}$$

54

where n_l is the size of the lth block and $\sum\limits_{u=1}^{n_l}$ denotes summation only in the lth block.

The simplest division of the ccd into orthogonal blocks is as follows:

Block 1: Factorial portion ($M = 2^k$ or 2^{k-m} points) plus n_F center point replicates.

Block 2: Axial portion ($2k$ points) plus n_A center point replicates. Application of (61) implies that the value of the axial settings is

$$\alpha = \sqrt{\frac{M(2k + n_A)}{2(M + n_F)}}. \tag{62}$$

For example, if $k = 3$ and $M = 2^3 = 8$, so that the first block contains the factorial arrangement plus n_F center point replicates and the second block contains a six-point octahedron plus n_A center point replicates, then

$$\alpha = \sqrt{\frac{4(6 + n_A)}{8 + n_F}}. \tag{63}$$

Now, if $n_F = 4$ center point replicates and $n_A = 0$, then $\alpha = \sqrt{2}$.

To achieve the rotatability property, the value of α must satisfy $\alpha = \sqrt[4]{M}$. In the example above, since $M = 8$, the value of α for rotatability is $\alpha = 1.682$. Although rotatability and orthogonal blocking for $k = 3$ cannot be achieved simultaneously, it is possible to come close to the rotatability property here by letting $n_F = n_A = 0$ and $\alpha = \sqrt{3} = 1.732$ or by letting $n_F = 4$, $n_A = 2$, so that $\alpha = \sqrt{8/3} = 1.633$. To achieve both properties simultaneously requires

$$M + n_F = \frac{\sqrt{M}}{2}(2k + n_A). \tag{64}$$

Table 11 lists blocking arrangements for the ccd for $k = 2, 3, \ldots, 6$ variables. When $k \geq 3$, it is possible to consider performing two or more blocks to accommodate the factorial (or cube) portion of the ccd. Each block will contain a 2^{k-m} fractional replicate for which the main effects of all of the factors must be estimable (i.e., the fractional factorials must be of resolution 3 or higher; see Box, Hunter, and Hunter (1978) for a discussion on design resolution). Each block used for the cube portion of the ccd must contain the same number of center point replicates.

A final word on the analysis of an orthogonally blocked ccd concerns the calculating formula and subsequent test for differences among the blocks. In the analysis of variance, the *sum of squares for blocks* is calculated using

$$\sum_{l=1}^{b}\frac{B_l^2}{n_l} - \frac{\left(\sum\limits_{u=1}^{N} Y_u\right)^2}{N} \tag{65}$$

where B_l is the total of the lth block and n_l is the number of units in the lth block. The sum of squares (65) has $b - 1$ degrees of freedom. The sum of squares for experimental error is the pooled sum of squares among the center point replicates in the same block. If the estimate of the error variance has ν degrees of freedom, then the test for zero differences among the blocks is the F ratio (Mean Square

Table 11
Some Blocking Arrangements for the CCD

	$k = 2$	3	4	5	5(½ rep)	6	6(½ rep)
Blocks within cube							
Number of points in cube	4	8	16	32	16	64	32
Number of blocks in cube	1	2	2	4	1	8	2
Number of center pt. reps. in each block	3	2	2	2	6	1	4
Axial block							
Number of axial pts.	4	6	8	10	10	12	12
n_A	3	2	2	4	1	6	2
Total number of observations (N)	14	20	30	54	33	90	54
α (orth. blocking)	1.4142	1.6330	2.000	2.3664	2.0000	2.8284	2.3664
α (rotatability)	1.4142	1.6818	2.000	2.3784	2.0000	2.8284	2.3784

Blocks)/(SS Experimental Error/ν) which is compared to the table value of F with $b - 1$ and ν degrees of freedom in the numerator and denominator, respectively.

4.3.1 An Example of an Orthogonally Blocked CCD in $k = 4$ Variables

Return to the process development study example of Section 3.2.1 where the data for the 16 factor-level combinations are listed in Table 7. The four factors studied are catalyst charge ($X_1 = $ lb), temperature ($X_2 = $ °C), pressure ($X_3 = $ psi), and concentration ($X_4 = $ %), on the response, conversion ($Y = $ %).

To illustrate the fitting of a second-degree model, the 2^4 factorial arrangement must be augmented with $2k = 8$ axial or "star" points plus some number, $n_0 \geq 1$, of center point replicates in order to produce the ccd. For the present, it will be assumed that the experiments are to be performed in blocks since the total number of experiments is $16 + 8 + n_0 = 24 + n_0$, which is too large to be performed under steady state conditions.

The experimental strategy suggested in Table 11, for $k = 4$, is to consider three blocks. The 16 factor-level combinations of the 2^4 factorial are divided into two blocks, eight combinations per block, with each block also containing $n_F = 2$ center point replicates. The division of the 16 combinations is performed by using two half replicates where the 2^{4-1} in block 1 is listed in Table 8. The eight axial points plus $n_A = 2$ center point replicates, make up the third block. The design array for this central composite design, where α is set equal to 2.0 to achieve the rotatability property as well as the orthogonal blocking property, is as follows:

	Block 1					Block 2					Block 3			
x_1	x_2	x_3	x_4		x_1	x_2	x_3	x_4		x_1	x_2	x_3	x_4	Y^+
-1	1	1	-1		1	-1	-1	-1		-2	0	0	0	69^+
1	1	-1	-1		-1	1	-1	-1		2	0	0	0	54^+
-1	-1	1	1		-1	-1	1	-1		0	-2	0	0	68^+
-1	-1	-1	-1		1	1	1	-1		0	2	0	0	51^+
1	-1	1	-1		-1	-1	-1	1		0	0	-2	0	73^+
1	1	1	1		1	1	-1	1		0	0	2	0	81^+
1	-1	-1	1		1	-1	1	1		0	0	0	-2	66^+
-1	1	-1	1		-1	1	1	1		0	0	0	2	68^+
0	0	0	0	89^+	0	0	0	0 97^+		0	0	0	0	83^+
0	0	0	0	95^+	0	0	0	0 93^+		0	0	0	0	80^+

$^+$ Artificial values of the response, conversion (%).

The experiments within a block should be performed in random order.

To show the calculations performed in computing the sum of squares for blocks using (65) as well as to compute the sum of squares for estimating the error variance for which to test for zero differences among the blocks, artificial data values (denoted by Y^+) have been introduced for the center point replicates in each of the three blocks as well as data values for the axial points in block 3. For the center point replicates in block 1, the conversion values are 89 and 95 so that the total for block 1 (the eight conversion values in Table 8 plus the center point replicates, 89 and 95) is $B_1 = 761$. The total for block 2 (the conversion values in Table 7 without the asterisks plus the center point replicates, 97 and 93) is $B_2 = 769$. The total of the conversion values in block 3 is $B_3 = 693$ so that the sum of squares for blocks is calculated as

$$\frac{B_1^2 + B_2^2 + B_3^2}{10} - \frac{(B_1 + B_2 + B_3)^2}{30} = \frac{761^2 + 769^2 + 693^2}{10} - \frac{(2223)^2}{30}$$
$$= 348.8 \text{ with 2 degrees of freedom.}$$

Using the three pairs of center point replicates, the pooled sum of squares for error is

$$\frac{(89 - 95)^2}{2} + \frac{(93 - 97)^2}{2} + \frac{(80 - 83)^2}{2} = 30.5 \text{ with } 1 + 1 + 1$$
$$= 3 \text{ degrees of freedom}$$

and the F-test for zero differences among the blocks is

$$F = \frac{348.8/2}{30.5/3} = 17.15 > F_{(2,3,0.05)} = 9.55$$

which implies the blocks are significantly different from each other.

To proceed now in fitting the second-degree model to the 30 data values (the 16 from Table 7 plus the 14 artificial values), with and without two block terms in the model, only the value of b_0 would be different with the two models. That is, inclusion of the block variables in the model does not affect the values of the estimated coefficients for the first- and second-degree terms.

4.4 Designs Other Than the CCD for Fitting Second-Degree Models

Although the central composite design is perhaps the most popular design for fitting a second-degree polynomial, there are other types of designs that are available. Specifically, the class of equiradial designs and Box-Behnken designs will be discussed.

4.4.1 Equiradial Designs

An equiradial design for fitting a second-degree model is a design consisting of two or more sets of points positioned on concentric circles, spheres, or hyperspheres of different radii. In each set the points are equispaced from one another as well as equidistant from the center of the design. Examples of second-order equiradial designs that are rotatable are concentric sets of points forming the vertices of regular polygons (pentagon, hexagon, octagon, etc.) in a plane, or polyhedrons in a three-dimensional space, or polytopes in higher-dimensional space. Several equiradial rotatable designs for the $k = 2$ and $k = 3$ cases only will be presented.

Two-Dimensional Designs, $k = 2$

In two dimensions, all the regular figures having five or more vertices, and each augmented with at least one center point, provide second-order rotatable designs. The choice of one design over another is usually determined by the number of experiments one wishes to perform as well as by the number of different levels for each factor one must maintain.

The simplest second order rotatable design in $k = 2$ dimensions is provided by the vertices of a pentagon with one or more points at the center of the design as illustrated in Figure 13a. Since the second-degree model for $k = 2$ variables contains six terms, replicate observations at one or more points of the design are required to obtain an estimate of the error variance. To ensure good predictability inside the experimental region, the center point should be replicated.

Illustrated in Figure 13b is the hexagonal design. The particular orientation of the hexagon in Figure 13b requires that x_1 be held at five equally spaced settings $(-1, -.5, 0, .5, 1)$ and that x_2 be held at three equally spaced settings $(-.866, 0, .866)$. Since the hexagonal design is rotatable, however, the points may be rotated to any other orientation without effecting the value of $\text{Var}[\hat{Y}(\mathbf{x})]$ for the second-degree fitted model.

Another desirable property of the hexagonal design in Figure 13b is that it blocks orthogonally. Vertices 1,3, and 5 form the vertices of an equilateral triangle (as do vertices 2, 4, and 6) or simplex in two dimensions and, as stated in Section 3.3, is a first-degree rotatable design. Thus, the hexagonal design can be broken into two blocks, each block having three peripheral points plus two center points.

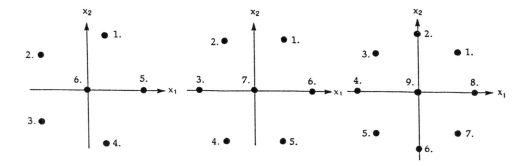

Figure 13
Some popular second-order rotatable designs and their design arrays: a. pentagonal design, b. hexagonal design, c. octagonal design, each with one center point

The center point is replicated within each block to provide a pooled estimate of the experimental error variance.

Still another useful rotatable second-order design (for $k = 2$) is the octagonal design with one or more center points as illustrated in Figure 13c. The particular orientation of the design point locations of the octagon in Figure 13c along with the center point are identical to the design point settings for a rotatable ccd with $\alpha = \sqrt{2}$. Thus, the octagonal design blocks orthogonally (even if the points are rotated slightly) using two blocks where the points 1, 3, 5, and 7 with two center point replicates are performed in block 1 and by grouping points 2, 4, 6, and 8 with two center point replicates to form block 2.

Three and Higher Dimensional Designs, $k \geqslant 3$.

In three dimensions, sets of points evenly spaced on a sphere are given by the vertices of five regular figures; the tetrahedron ($n = 4$), the octahedron ($n = 6$), the cube ($n = 8$), the icosahedron ($n = 12$), and the dodecahedron ($n = 20$). The vertices of the tetrahedron $(1, -1, -1)$, $(-1, 1, -1)$, $(-1, -1, 1)$, and $(1, 1, 1)$; the vertices of the octahedron $(\pm \sqrt{3}, 0, 0)$, $(0, \pm \sqrt{3}, 0)$, $(0, 0, \pm \sqrt{3})$; and the vertices of the cube $(\pm 1, \pm 1, \pm 1)$, do not individually support a rotatable design of order 2 (they do support a rotatable design of order 1), but they may be combined to give a second-order rotatable design.

The icosahedron and the dodecahedron, when augmented with center point replicates, are second-order rotatable designs. The combination of the cube plus the octahedron (with $\sqrt{3}$ replaced by 1.682) and one or more center point replicates, produces the CCD, which is a rotatable second-order design. This is also true, of course, for $k \geqslant 4$. The design array consisting of the cube plus octahedron, with one center point, for $k = 3$, is

	Cube		Octahedron and Center Point		
x_1	x_2	x_3	x_1	x_2	x_3
-1	-1	-1			
1	-1	-1	-1.682	0	0
-1	1	-1	1.682	0	0
1	1	-1	0	-1.682	0
-1	-1	1	0	1.682	0
1	-1	1	0	0	-1.682
-1	1	1	0	0	1.682
1	1	1	0	0	0

4.4.2 Box-Behnken Designs

Box and Behnken (1960) suggest how to select a fraction of the 3^k factorial arrangement which allows efficient estimation of the first- and second-order coefficients in model (59). The levels of each of the k quantitative factors are assumed equally spaced so that the values of the coded x_i are -1, 0, and 1.

The designs are formed by combining two-level factorial arrangements with incomplete block designs in a particular manner. To illustrate, take $k = 4$ variables and assign them, two at a time, in six blocks of size 2, that is,

Block	Variables	
1	x_1	x_2
2	x_3	x_4
3	x_1	x_3
4	x_2	x_4
5	x_1	x_4
6	x_2	x_3

Now, with each pair of variables in a block, set up a 2^2 factorial arrangement in the specific variables, and set the levels of the remaining variables equal to zero, then

Block	x_1	x_2	x_3	x_4
1	± 1	± 1	0	0
2	0	0	± 1	± 1
3	± 1	0	± 1	0
4	0	± 1	0	± 1
5	± 1	0	0	± 1
6	0	± 1	± 1	0

If blocks 1 and 2, 3 and 4, and 5 and 6 are now combined to form three new blocks each of size 8 and one or more center points is added to each of the three blocks, the design array for the fraction of the 3^4 factorial in three blocks of nine experimental units each is

x_1	x_2	x_3	x_4	
± 1	± 1	0	0	
0	0	± 1	± 1	Block 1
0	0	0	0	(9 rows)
± 1	0	± 1	0	
0	± 1	0	± 1	Block 2
0	0	0	0	(9 rows)
± 1	0	0	± 1	
0	± 1	± 1	0	Block 3
0	0	0	0	(9 rows)

This design is a rotatable second-order design and blocks orthogonally so that the first- and second-order coefficients in the second-degree model are not affected by the differences in blocks 1, 2, and 3.

Box and Behnken present a list of ten designs covering values of $k = 3, 4, 5, 6, 7, 9, 10, 11, 12,$ and 16. Associated with each design is the blocking arrangement if the design blocks orthogonally. Also presented are the formulas for calculating the coefficient estimates in the second-degree fitted model and for computing the sums of squares (due to the linear terms and due to the second-degree terms) in the analysis of variance. Data from a four-factor experiment is used to illustrate the calculations.

5

Response surface methodology consists of a set of techniques used in the empirical study of relationships between one or more measured quality responses such as yield, coating thickness, and tensile strength, on the one hand, and a number of input variables (or factors) such as temperature, pressure, and concentration of the ingredients, on the other. The techniques are used to answer such questions as: **5.0 Summary**

1. How is the particular response influenced by the given set of input variables over some specified region of interest?
2. Can an *optimal value* of the response in the selected region of experimentation be found? If so, what are the settings of the input variables that produce the optimal response and what is the shape of the response surface in the neighborhood of this optimum?
3. If an optimal value of the response is not discovered in the region of interest, what changes are necessary in terms of input variable selection or selection of the region of experimentation to guarantee a more successful program of experimentation?

In this booklet, questions 1 and 2 were primarily addressed. Section 1 introduced the subject of response surface methodology by listing some of the terminology that is used and discussing the objectives sought and assumptions made when modeling a response surface. Section 2 presented the steps taken in a sequential approach in searching for the settings of the input variables that yield the optimal response value. The steps involve:

1. Fitting the *simplest form of polynomial,* usually a first-degree polynomial, and testing for adequacy of fit.
2. Using the first-degree fitted model to *locate higher values* of the response along the path of steepest ascent.
3. In a region where *nonplanarity* in the surface is present, fitting additional terms such as crossproduct terms and/or pure quadratic terms to produce the second-degree model.

4. Using the second-degree model to *map or describe the shape of the response surface* in the experimental region. If it is further determined that the optimal or best value of the response is within the boundaries of the region, then an attempt is made to *locate the settings of the input variables* that yield the optimal value of the response.

To illustrate the four steps of the sequential procedure, an example is presented of a manufacturing process that produces plastic disks, where disk thickness is the measured response of interest.

   Sections 3 and 4 presented some of the more popular designs used for collecting data for fitting the first- and second-degree polynomials. Two-level factorial arrangements, fractions of the 2^k, simplex designs, and Plackett-Burman designs are singled out as useful first-order designs. These designs are easily augmented to form the second-order central composite designs and the equiradial designs of Section 4 for fitting second-degree models. The augmentation can be achieved in

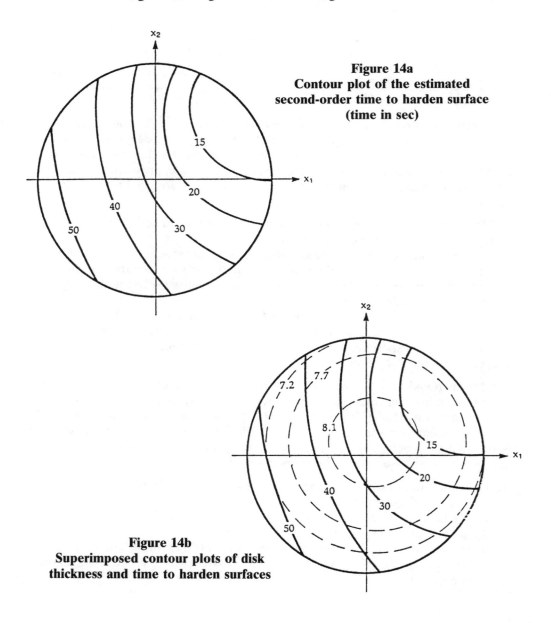

Figure 14a
Contour plot of the estimated second-order time to harden surface (time in sec)

Figure 14b
Superimposed contour plots of disk thickness and time to harden surfaces

the face of changing experimental conditions by considering the orthogonal blocking scheme discussed in Section 4.3.

In this booklet, little attention has been given to the use of transformations applied either to the response or to the values of the predictor variables, except in the case of the predictor variables where coded variables were defined in Section 2. Sometimes the units of measurement in the response as well as in the predictor variables may not be the units in which the system is most simply modeled. Box and Draper (1987) devote an entire chapter (Chapter 8) to discussing the use of transformations both on the response and on the predictor variables for not only simplifying the complexity of the system but also for validating distributional assumptions.

Response surface methodology is an interesting and challenging area for studying process optimization. Only the tip of the response surface iceberg has been uncovered in this booklet. As an example of the brevity of coverage, in each of the examples presented only a single response variable was considered. Often times, however, the experimenter is actually interested in finding a region which is optimum, not for just a single response, but for two or more responses simultaneously. For example, in the disk manufacturing process, suppose that in addition to maximizing disk thickness (Y_1), one desires to minimize the time required to mold the disks. If the variable, time to hardening (Y_2), is a response variable (unlike time kept in mold which is a controllable factor) and is modeled using a second-degree model in X_1 (f/e) and X_2 (cm) which is fitted to the points of the ccd in Figure 6b, then the contour plot of the hardening time surface as displayed in Figure 14a can be visualized. In an attempt to locate the combinations of the values of X_1 and X_2 that produce thick disks ($Y_1 \geqslant 8.1$, e.g.) while at the same time require a minimum length of time to harden ($Y_2 \leqslant 15$ secs, say), one can superimpose the two contour plots of Figures 6b and 14a, as shown in Figure 14b. The analysis of multiresponse experiments is presented in Chapter 7 of Khuri and Cornell (1987).

Many other strategies for process optimization exist such as the Nelder-Mead (1965) Simplex Method, which is an optimization procedure by direct search without the use of a response equation, the method of ridge analysis presented by Draper (1963), and Evolutionary Operation (EVOP) by Box and Draper (1969), to name just a few. Optimization of multiresponse processes (such as considered in Figure 14b) and model discrimination have also received some attention in the literature and it is my hope that these areas will be discussed in future volumes of this booklet series.

Box, G. E. P. and D. W. Behnken. Some New Three–Level Designs for the Study of Quantitative Variables. *Technometrics* 2 (1960):455–475. Discusses how to construct fractional replicates of the 3^k factorials so the resulting designs are approximately rotatable and for the most part can be orthogonally blocked.

Box, G. E. P. and N. R. Draper. *Evolutionary Operation*. New York: Wiley and Sons, Inc. (1969). An introductory book, written mainly for industrial management, on how EVOP can be performed on industrial processes. Also discusses experimental design and analysis on a practitioner's level.

Box, G. E. P. and N. R. Draper. Robust Designs. *Biometrika* 62 (1975):347–352. Discusses desirable properties of response surface designs with an emphasis on the robustness to outliers and nonnormality.

Box, G. E. P. and N. R. Draper. *Empirical Model-Building and Response Surfaces*. New York: Wiley and Sons, Inc. (1987). Written by two practitioners and active researchers who are in the forefront of response surface methods, this book begins from first principles and logically develops basic ideas, finally moving to a discussion of important research findings.

Box, G. E. P., W. G. Hunter, and J. S. Hunter. *Statistics for Experimenters: An Introduction to Design, Data Analysis, and Model Building*. New York: Wiley and Sons, Inc. (1978). An intermediate level book on experimental design and analysis as well as model building, written with the nonstatistician in mind, emphasizing applications in the physical, engineering, biological, and social sciences.

Box, G. E. P. and K. B. Wilson. On the Experimental Attainment of Optimum Conditions. *Journal of the Royal Statistical Society* B, 13 (1951):1–45. A lucid presentation on the exploration of a yield surface generated by a chemical process. Composite designs for fitting second-degree polynomials were first introduced in this paper.

Bradley, R. A. Determination of Optimum Operating Conditions by Experimental Methods: Part I, Mathematics and Statistics Fundamental to the Fitting of Response Surfaces. *Industrial Quality Control,* July (1958):16–20. An introduction to the analysis of first-degree models fitted to factorial fractional arrangements with additional comments leading to setting up the canonical form of the second-degree surface.

Connor, W. S. and M. Zelen. Fractional Factorial Experimental Designs for Factors at Three Levels. National Bureau of Standards, Washington, D.C., Applied Mathematics Series, No. 54 (1959). A catalogue of 3^{k-m} fractional factorial design plans.

Cornell, J. A. *How to Run Mixture Experiments for Product Quality,* Vol 5. 2nd ed. Milwaukee, WI: American Society for Quality Control (1990). Discusses how to set up designs, what types of model forms to use, and ways of interpreting the analysis of data collected from mixture experiments.

Cornell, J. A., J. T. Shelton, R. Lynch, and G. F. Piepel. Plotting Three-Dimensional Response Surfaces for Three-Component Mixtures or Two-Factor Systems. *Florida Agricultural Experiment Station, Bulletin No. 836,* (1983). Discusses the use of SAS/GRAPH for plotting three-dimensional response surfaces and surface contours.

Davies, O. L. *The Design and Analysis of Industrial Experiments*. New York: Hafner Publishing Company (1960). An intermediate level text on statistical designs and the analysis of experimental data with an industrial slant.

Draper, N. R. Ridge Analysis of Response Surfaces. *Technometrics* 5 (1963):469–

479. A method for finding the optimal response on concentric circles centered at the center of the design.

Hahn, G. J. Experimental Design in the Complex World. *Technometrics* 26 (1984):19–31. A lucid presentation of the basic guidelines used for designing experiments. Examples of six different experiments are used to illustrate the concepts presented.

Hicks, C. R. *Fundamental Concepts in the Design of Experiments*. New York: Holt, Rinehart, and Winston (1963). An introductory book on experimental design and the analysis of experiments.

Hunter, J. S. Determination of Optimum Operating Conditions by Experimental Methods: Part II-1, Models and Methods. *Industrial Quality Control*. December (1958):16–24.

Hunter, J. S. Part II-2, Models and Methods. *Industrial Quality Control*. January (1959a):7–15.

Hunter, J. S. Part II-3, Models and Methods. *Industrial Quality Control*. February (1959b):6–14. A three-paper series that guides the reader through the various stages of a complete response surface investigation. First- and second-order designs are presented, first- and second-degree models are fitted, with emphasis placed on the analysis of data. The techniques are illustrated in detail using data representing the yield of a chemical process.

Khuri, A. I. and J. A. Cornell. *Response Surfaces: Designs and Analyses*. New York: Marcel Dekker, Inc. (1987). An up-to-date text covering standard response surface designs and methods of analysis along with more specialized topics such as the analysis of multiresponse experiments and nonlinear response surface models.

Montgomery, D. C. *Design and Analysis of Experiments*. New York: Wiley and Sons, Inc. (1976). An intermediate level text on statistical designs and the analysis of experimental data.

Myers, R. H. *Response Surface Methodology*. Boston: Allyn and Bacon, Inc. (1976). (Distributed by Edwards Brothers, Inc., Ann Arbor, MI.) The first book devoted specifically to the application of response surface methods.

Nelder, J. A. and R. Mead. A Simplex Method for Function Minimization Problems. *The Computer Journal* 7 (1965):308–313. Discusses a derivative-free approach to function minimization by flipping the vertices of a k-dimensional simplex.

Plackett, R. L. and J. P. Burman. The Design of Optimum Multifactorial Experiments. *Biometrika* 33(1946):305–325.

SAS Institute, *SAS User's Guide: Statistics*. Cary, NC: SAS Institute (1982).

**Appendix A:
A Brief Review
of the Method of
Least Squares
and Its Properties
Using Matrix
Notation**

In matrix notation, the first-degree model of Equation 10 over the N observations, can be expressed as

$$\mathbf{Y} = \mathbf{X}\boldsymbol{\beta} + \boldsymbol{\epsilon} \tag{A1}$$

where

$$\mathbf{Y} = \begin{bmatrix} Y_1 \\ Y_2 \\ \cdot \\ \cdot \\ \cdot \\ Y_N \end{bmatrix}, \; \mathbf{X} = \begin{bmatrix} 1 & x_{11} & x_{12} & \cdots & x_{1k} \\ 1 & x_{21} & x_{22} & \cdots & x_{2k} \\ \cdot & \cdot & \cdot & & \cdot \\ \cdot & \cdot & \cdot & & \cdot \\ \cdot & \cdot & \cdot & & \cdot \\ 1 & x_{N1} & x_{N2} & \cdots & x_{Nk} \end{bmatrix}, \; \boldsymbol{\beta} = \begin{bmatrix} \beta_0 \\ \beta_1 \\ \cdot \\ \cdot \\ \cdot \\ \beta_k \end{bmatrix}, \; \boldsymbol{\epsilon} = \begin{bmatrix} \epsilon_1 \\ \epsilon_2 \\ \cdot \\ \cdot \\ \cdot \\ \epsilon_N \end{bmatrix}.$$

$$Nx1 \qquad\qquad Nx(k+1) \qquad\qquad (k+1)x1 \qquad Nx1$$

The normal equations are

$$\mathbf{X}'\mathbf{X}\mathbf{b} = \mathbf{X}'\mathbf{Y} \tag{A2}$$

where the $(k+1)x(k+1)$ square matrix $\mathbf{X}'\mathbf{X}$ consists of sums of squares and sums of crossproducts of the factor levels and the $(k+1)x1$ vector $\mathbf{X}'\mathbf{Y}$ consists of sums of crossproducts of the x_{ui} and Y_u. The least squares estimates of the elements of $\boldsymbol{\beta}$ are given by the solution of Equation A2 for $\mathbf{b}$ which is

$$\mathbf{b} = (\mathbf{X}'\mathbf{X})^{-1}\mathbf{X}'\mathbf{Y} \tag{A3}$$

where the matrix $(\mathbf{X}'\mathbf{X})^{-1}$ is the inverse of $\mathbf{X}'\mathbf{X}$. Since $\mathbf{X}'\mathbf{X}$ is symmetric, so is $(\mathbf{X}'\mathbf{X})^{-1}$. Note that it is assumed here that $\mathbf{X}$ in Equation A1 is of full column rank.

A.1 Properties of the Coefficient Estimates

The statistical properties of the estimator $\mathbf{b}$ are easily verified once assumptions are made concerning the elements of $\boldsymbol{\epsilon}$. Writing the expectation of the elements of the random error vector in equation A1 to be $E(\boldsymbol{\epsilon}) = 0$ and $\text{Var}(\boldsymbol{\epsilon}) = E[\boldsymbol{\epsilon}\boldsymbol{\epsilon}'] = \sigma^2\mathbf{I}_N$, (i.e., the errors are assumed to have a zero mean, the same variance, and are uncorrelated), where $\mathbf{I}_N$ is the identity matrix of order N, the expectation of $\mathbf{b}$ is

$$\begin{aligned}
E[\mathbf{b}] &= E[(\mathbf{X}'\mathbf{X})^{-1}\mathbf{X}'\mathbf{Y}] \\
&= E[(\mathbf{X}'\mathbf{X})^{-1}\mathbf{X}'(\mathbf{X}\boldsymbol{\beta} + \boldsymbol{\epsilon})] \\
&= \boldsymbol{\beta} + E[(\mathbf{X}'\mathbf{X})^{-1}\mathbf{X}'\boldsymbol{\epsilon}] \\
&= \boldsymbol{\beta}.
\end{aligned} \tag{A4}$$

In other words if the model $\mathbf{Y} = \mathbf{X}\boldsymbol{\beta} + \boldsymbol{\epsilon}$ is correct, then $\mathbf{b}$ is an *unbiased estimator* of $\boldsymbol{\beta}$, otherwise the estimates are biased as shown in Section A.5.

The variance-covariance matrix of the elements of $\mathbf{b}$ is expressed as

$$\begin{aligned}
\text{Var}(\mathbf{b}) &= \text{Var}[(\mathbf{X}'\mathbf{X})^{-1}\mathbf{X}'\mathbf{Y}] \\
&= (\mathbf{X}'\mathbf{X})^{-1}\mathbf{X}' \ \text{Var}(\mathbf{Y})\mathbf{X}(\mathbf{X}'\mathbf{X})^{-1}.
\end{aligned}$$

Since $\text{Var}(\mathbf{Y}) = \text{Var}(\boldsymbol{\epsilon}) = \sigma^2\mathbf{I}_N$, then

$$\text{Var}(\mathbf{b}) = (\mathbf{X}'\mathbf{X})^{-1}\sigma^2. \tag{A5}$$

Along the main diagonal of the matrix $\mathbf{C}\sigma^2 = (\mathbf{X}'\mathbf{X})^{-1}\sigma^2$, the iith element, $c_{ii}\sigma^2$, is the variance of b_i, the ith element of $\mathbf{b}$. The ijth element of $\mathbf{C}$, $c_{ij}\sigma^2$, is the covariance between the elements b_i and b_j of $\mathbf{b}$. The standard error of b_i is the positive square root of the variance of b_i and is $\sqrt{c_{ii}\sigma^2}$. Furthermore, if the errors $\boldsymbol{\epsilon}$ are jointly normally distributed, then the distribution of $\mathbf{b}$ is written as

$$\mathbf{b} \sim N(\boldsymbol{\beta}, (\mathbf{X}'\mathbf{X})^{-1}\sigma^2). \tag{A6}$$

A.2 Predicted Response Values

Once the vector of estimates $\mathbf{b}$ is obtained using Equation A3, the predicted value of the response at any point $\mathbf{x} = (x_1, x_2, \ldots, x_k)'$ in the experimental region is expressed in matrix notation as

$$\hat{Y}(\mathbf{x}) = \mathbf{x}_p'\mathbf{b} \tag{A7}$$

where $\mathbf{x}_p'$ is a $1 \times p$ vector whose elements correspond to the elements in a row of the matrix $\mathbf{X}$ but where the values of the elements in the row of $\mathbf{X}$ are specified in $\mathbf{x}$. In Equation A7, $p = k + 1$. Specifically, if the predicted value of the response corresponding to the uth observation is desired, then $\hat{Y}_u = \hat{Y}(\mathbf{x}) = \mathbf{x}_u'\mathbf{b}$, where $\mathbf{x}_u'$ is the uth row of $\mathbf{X}$. [We use the notation $\hat{Y}(\mathbf{x})$ to denote the predicted value of Y at the point $\mathbf{x}$.]

A measure of the precision of the estimate $\hat{Y}(\mathbf{x})$, defined as the variance of $\hat{Y}(\mathbf{x})$, is expressed as

$$\text{Var}[\hat{Y}(\mathbf{x})] = \text{Var}[\mathbf{x}_p'\mathbf{b}]$$
$$= \mathbf{x}_p' \text{Var}(\mathbf{b})\mathbf{x}_p$$
$$= \mathbf{x}_p'(\mathbf{X}'\mathbf{X})^{-1}\mathbf{x}_p\sigma^2. \tag{A8}$$

The standard error of $\hat{Y}(\mathbf{x})$ is $\sqrt{\text{Var}[\hat{Y}(\mathbf{x})]}$. The inverse matrix $(\mathbf{X}'\mathbf{X})^{-1}$ used for obtaining $\mathbf{b}$ in Equation A3 also determines the variances and covariances of the elements of $\mathbf{b}$ as well as the variance of $\hat{Y}(\mathbf{x})$.

A.3 Residuals

The difference between the observed value of the response at the uth trial and the value predicted with the fitted model for the uth trial is known as the uth residual, $r_u = Y_u - \hat{Y}_u$, for $u = 1, 2, \ldots, N$. If predicted values are obtained for each of the N trials, then the vector of residuals is $\mathbf{r} = (r_1, r_2, \ldots, r_N)' = \mathbf{Y} - \mathbf{Xb}$. It is important to distinguish between the errors ϵ_u of the Y_u with respect to the corresponding true values η in $Y_u = \eta + \epsilon_u$ and the residuals r_u of the Y_u with respect to the predicted values $\hat{Y}_u$. Some comments on how to use residuals to check on the assumptions of normality and of constant variance are given in Cornell (1990): 30.

Several properties of the residuals are worth mentioning here. When the model to be fitted, as in Equation A3, contains a β_0 term, then the sum of the N residuals equals zero, that is, $\Sigma_{u=1}^{N} r_u = 0$. Furthermore, the sum of the products $r_u \hat{Y}_u$ equals zero, and the sum of the products $r_u x_{ui}$ equals zero, for each $i = 1, 2, \ldots, k$. In matrix notation these properties are

i. $\mathbf{1}'\mathbf{r} = 0$ where $\mathbf{1}'$ is a $1 \times N$ vector of ones
ii. $\hat{\mathbf{Y}}'\mathbf{r} = 0$
iii. $\mathbf{X}'\mathbf{r} = 0$.

A.4 Estimation of σ^2

In the formula (A5) for the variance-covariance matrix of the estimates $\mathbf{b}$ as well as the formula in Equation A8 for the variance of $\hat{Y}(\mathbf{x})$, the variance, σ^2, of the errors was assumed known. This is seldom the case, however, and usually an estimate of σ^2 needs to be calculated during the analysis of the data values. For the general case where the fitted model contains p terms and the total number of observations is N ($N > p$), an estimate, s^2, of σ^2 is computed from

$$s^2 = \frac{1}{N-p} \sum_{u=1}^{N} r_u^2$$

$$= \frac{1}{N-p} (\mathbf{Y} - \mathbf{Xb})'(\mathbf{Y} - \mathbf{Xb})$$

$$= \frac{1}{N-p} \text{SSE} \tag{A9}$$

where SSE is called the sum of squared residuals. The divisor N-p is called the degrees of freedom of the estimator s^2. When the true model is given by $\mathbf{Y} = \mathbf{X}\boldsymbol{\beta} + \boldsymbol{\epsilon}$ then s^2 is an unbiased estimator of σ^2.

A.5 Biases in the Coefficient Estimates When the Fitted Model is an Underestimate of the True Surface

Suppose the true response surface can be expressed in the coded variables as

$$\mathbf{Y} = \mathbf{X}\boldsymbol{\beta} + \mathbf{X}_2\boldsymbol{\beta}_2 + \boldsymbol{\epsilon} \tag{A10}$$

where the elements of the matrix $\mathbf{X}_2$ consist of higher degree terms in the x_is than are contained in $\mathbf{X}$ and the elements of the vector $\boldsymbol{\beta}_2$ are the coefficients of the higher degree terms. For example, if the true surface is of the second degree in the k variables, then the $k(k + 1)/2$ elements in the uth row ($1 \leq u \leq N$) of $\mathbf{X}_2$ are x_{u1}^2, $x_{u2}^2, \ldots, x_{uk}^2, x_{u1}x_{u2}, \ldots, x_{uk-1}x_{uk}$ and the elements of $\boldsymbol{\beta}_2$ are $\beta_{11}, \beta_{22}, \ldots, \beta_{kk}, \beta_{12}, \ldots, \beta_{k-1k}$.

With the fitted model of the form (A1), the formula (A3) used for calculating the estimates of the coefficients $\mathbf{b}$, produces *biased estimates*. The amount of bias in the estimates is expressible as $(\mathbf{X}'\mathbf{X})^{-1}\mathbf{X}'\mathbf{X}_2\boldsymbol{\beta}_2$ since

$$
\begin{aligned}
E(\mathbf{b}) &= (\mathbf{X}'\mathbf{X})^{-1}\mathbf{X}'E(\mathbf{Y}) \\
&= (\mathbf{X}'\mathbf{X})^{-1}\mathbf{X}'[\mathbf{X}\boldsymbol{\beta} + \mathbf{X}_2\boldsymbol{\beta}_2] \\
&= \boldsymbol{\beta} + (\mathbf{X}'\mathbf{X})^{-1}\mathbf{X}'\mathbf{X}_2\boldsymbol{\beta}_2.
\end{aligned} \tag{A11}
$$

The matrix $(\mathbf{X}'\mathbf{X})^{-1}\mathbf{X}'\mathbf{X}_2$ is called the *alias matrix* and the elements of the alias matrix are functions of the coordinates of the design array which appear in the matrix $\mathbf{X}$ as well as the elements of $\mathbf{X}_2$.

To illustrate the bias expressions for the coefficient estimates in the first-degree fitted model, let $k = 2$ and suppose the simplex design of Figure 11a is used to fit the model $Y = \beta_0 + \beta_1 x_1 + \beta_2 x_2 + \epsilon$. Over $N = 3$ observations, the $\mathbf{X}$ matrix is

$$
\mathbf{X} = \begin{bmatrix} 1 & -\sqrt{3/2} & -1/\sqrt{2} \\ 1 & \sqrt{3/2} & -1/\sqrt{2} \\ 1 & 0 & \sqrt{2} \end{bmatrix}.
$$

Let us assume the true surface is of the second degree, $E(Y) = \beta_0 + \beta_1 x_1 + \beta_2 x_2 + \beta_{11}x_1^2 + \beta_{22}x_2^2 + \beta_{12}x_1 x_2$, so that the elements of the matrix $\mathbf{X}_2$ and the vector $\boldsymbol{\beta}_2$ are

$$
\mathbf{X}_2 = \begin{bmatrix} 3/2 & 1/2 & \sqrt{3/2} \\ 3/2 & 1/2 & -\sqrt{3/2} \\ 0 & 2 & 0 \end{bmatrix}, \quad \boldsymbol{\beta}_2 = \begin{bmatrix} \beta_{11} \\ \beta_{22} \\ \beta_{12} \end{bmatrix}.
$$

Then the form of the alias matrix is

$$
(\mathbf{X}'\mathbf{X})^{-1}\mathbf{X}'\mathbf{X}_2 = \begin{bmatrix} 3 & 3 & 0 \\ 0 & 0 & -3/\sqrt{2} \\ -3/\sqrt{2} & 3/\sqrt{2} & 0 \end{bmatrix}
$$

and the expectations of the elements in **b** are

$$E(b_0) = \beta_0 + 3(\beta_{11} + \beta_{22})$$
$$E(b_1) = \beta_1 - (3/\sqrt{2})\beta_{12} \tag{A12}$$
$$E(b_2) = \beta_2 + (3/\sqrt{2})(\beta_{22} - \beta_{11}).$$

In other words, in fitting a first-degree model to data collected at the points of a first-order design when in fact the true surface is of a degree higher than one, the estimates of the coefficients in the first-degree model are biased by the higher-degree measures (β_{11}, β_{22}, and β_{12}) of nonplanarity of the true surface. The particular expressions for the bias in (A12) are functions of the design (Figure 11a) as well as the elements of $\boldsymbol{\beta}_2$ in (A10).

**Appendix B:
Formulas for
Calculating the
Coefficient
Estimates in a
Second-Degree
Model Using a
Central
Composite
Design**

The central composite design (ccd) in k variables consists of the following sets of points,

   i. a two-level factorial arrangement (2^k or a suitable fraction, 2^{k-m} say)
      $(x_1, x_2, \ldots, x_k) = (\pm 1, \pm 1, \ldots, \pm 1)$
   ii. $2k$ axial or "star" points
      $(x_1, x_2, \ldots, x_k) = (\pm \alpha, 0, 0, \ldots, 0), (0, \pm \alpha, 0, \ldots, 0), \ldots, (0, 0, 0, \ldots, \pm \alpha)$
   iii. n_0 center points
      $(x_1, x_2, \ldots, x_k) = (0, 0, \ldots, 0)$.

The total number of distinct design points is $n = 2^k + 2k + 1$ or $2^{k-m} + 2k + 1$, (if $n_0 = 1$). Sometimes replicate observations (r of them) are collected at the factorial settings. In this case, the total number of observations is $N = M + 2k + n_0$ where $M = r\, 2^k$ or $r\, 2^{k-m}$.

The second-degree model in k variables fitted to data collected at the points of a ccd is

$$Y = \beta_0 + \sum_{i=1}^{k} \beta_i x_i + \sum_{i=1}^{k} \beta_{ii} x_i^2 + \sum_{i<j}^{k}\sum \beta_{ij} x_i x_j + \epsilon. \tag{B1}$$

Let us define the following sets of observations collected at the above sets of points of the ccd

   i. $Y_1, Y_2, \ldots, Y_M$ collected at the factorial portion ($x_i = \pm 1$)
   ii. Y_{M+2i-1}, Y_{M+2i} collected at the axial settings $x_i = \pm \alpha$, $x_i = 0, j \neq i$
   iii. $Y_{M+2k+1}, \ldots, Y_N$ collected at the center point $x_i = 0$, all i.

Then the formulas for calculating the estimates b_0, b_i, b_{ii}, and b_{ij} of the coefficients β_0, β_i, β_{ii}, and β_{ij}, respectively, in the model (B1), are

$$b_0 = \frac{2\alpha^2(\alpha^2 - k)}{D} \sum_{u=1}^{M} Y_u + \frac{M(K - \alpha^2)}{D} \sum_{u=M+1}^{M+2k} Y_u + \frac{(2\alpha^4 + Mk)}{D} \sum_{u=M+2k+1}^{N} Y_u$$

$$b_i = \frac{1}{(M + 2\alpha^2)} \sum_{u=1}^{M} x_{ui} Y_u + \frac{\alpha}{(M + 2\alpha^2)} (Y_{M+2i} - Y_{M+2i-1}) \quad 1 \leq i \leq k \tag{B2}$$

$$b_{ii} = \frac{-(M + 2\alpha^2)}{D} \sum_{u=1}^{N} Y_u + \frac{1}{2\alpha^4} \left[\sum_{u=1}^{M} Y_u + \alpha^2 (Y_{M+2i} - Y_{M+2i-1}) \right]$$

$$+ \frac{(M + 2\alpha^2)^2}{2\alpha^4 D} \left[k \sum_{u=1}^{M} Y_u + \alpha^2 \sum_{u=M+1}^{M+2k} Y_u \right]$$

$$b_{ij} = \frac{1}{M} \sum_{u=1}^{M} x_{ui} x_{uj} Y_u \quad 1 \leqslant i < j \leqslant k$$

where $D = (2\alpha^4 + Mk)N - (M + 2\alpha^2)^2 k$.

If the design is rotatable, the value of α is

$$\alpha = \sqrt[4]{M}$$

and the formulas in (B2) are further simplified to

$$b_0 = \frac{2(1 - k/\sqrt{M})}{D^*} \sum_{u=1}^{M} Y_u + \frac{(k - \sqrt{M})}{D^*} \sum_{u=M+1}^{M+2k} Y_u + \frac{(k + 2)}{D^*} \sum_{u=M+2k+1}^{N} Y_u$$

$$b_i = \frac{1}{H^*} \sum_{u=1}^{M} x_{ui} Y_u + \frac{\sqrt[4]{M}}{H^*} (Y_{M+2i} - Y_{M+2i-1}) \quad 1 \leqslant i \leqslant k$$

$$b_{ii} = \frac{(N\text{-}M\text{-}2\sqrt{M})}{MD^*} \sum_{u=1}^{M} Y_u + \frac{(M + 2\sqrt{M}\text{-}N)}{2\sqrt{M}\, D^*} \sum_{u=M+1}^{M+2k} Y_u - \frac{(1 + 2/\sqrt{M})}{D^*} \sum_{u=M+2k+1}^{N} Y_u$$

$$+ \frac{1}{2\sqrt{M}} (Y_{M+2i} + Y_{M+2i-1}) \tag{B3}$$

$$b_{ij} = \frac{1}{M} \sum_{u=1}^{M} x_{ui} x_{uj} Y_u \quad 1 \leqslant i < j \leqslant k$$

where $D^* = N(k + 2) - (2 + \sqrt{M})^2 k$ and $H^* = M + 2\sqrt{M}$.

**Appendix C:
Some 2^{k-m}
Fractional
Replicate
Arrangements for
$k = 3, 4, 5, 6$,
and $m = 1, 2$**

$k = 3$, $m = 1$:

$x_3 = -x_1 x_2$				$x_3 = x_1 x_2$		
x_1	x_2	x_3	or	x_1	x_2	x_3
-1	-1	-1		1	1	1
1	1	-1		-1	-1	1
1	-1	1		-1	1	-1
-1	1	1		1	-1	-1

$k = 4$, $m = 1$:

$x_4 = x_1 x_2 x_3$				$x_4 = x_1 x_2$				$x_4 = x_2 x_3$			
x_1	x_2	x_3	x_4	x_1	x_2	x_3	x_4	x_1	x_2	x_3	x_4
-1	-1	-1	-1	-1	-1	-1	1	-1	-1	-1	1
1	-1	-1	1	1	-1	-1	-1	1	-1	-1	1
-1	1	-1	1	-1	1	-1	-1	-1	1	-1	-1
1	1	-1	-1	1	1	-1	1	1	1	-1	-1
-1	-1	1	1	-1	-1	1	1	-1	-1	1	-1
1	-1	1	-1	1	-1	1	-1	1	-1	1	-1
-1	1	1	-1	-1	1	1	-1	-1	1	1	1
1	1	1	1	1	1	1	1	1	1	1	1

$k = 5$, $m = 1$: Write a complete 2^4 array in x_1, x_2, x_3, and x_4. Let $x_5 = x_1 x_2 x_3 x_4$ or $x_5 = -x_1 x_2 x_3 x_4$.

      $m = 2$: Write a complete 2^3 array in x_1, x_2, and x_3. Let $x_4 = x_1 x_2$ and $x_5 = x_1 x_3$.

$k = 6$, $m = 1$: Write a complete 2^5 array in x_1, x_2, x_3, x_4, and x_5. Let $x_6 = x_1 x_2 x_3 x_4 x_5$.

      $m = 2$: Write a complete 2^4 array in x_1, x_2, x_3, and x_4. Let $x_5 = x_1 x_2 x_3$ and $x_6 = x_1 x_3 x_4$; or $x_5 = -x_1 x_2 x_3$ and $x_6 = x_1 x_3 x_4$.

A complete table of two-level fractional factorial designs in $k = 3, 4, \ldots, 11$ variables using up to $N = 128$ experiments is given in Box, Hunter, and Hunter (1978): 410.

Unbiased estimator, 70
Units of measurement, 65

Value
    artificial data, 57
    of coded variables, 41, 53
    conversion, 46, 57
    predicted, 40, 52
    See also Coefficient; Predicted
  response value; response value.
Variable
    blocking, 2
    coded, 12, 14, 15, 24–26, 29, 31,
      34, 39, 40–42, 44, 49, 60, 65
    controllable, 22
    dependent, 2
    design, 39
    explanatory, 2
    independent, 11
    input, 63, 64
    predictor, 65
    regressor, 2
    response, 2, 8, 9, 16, 65

Variance
    of distribution, 18
    of estimated coefficients, 14, 16,
      48
    of error, 12, 20, 25–27, 40, 42, 71
    of estimated error, 19, 20, 30, 40,
      49, 55, 57, 59
    of fitted model, 40
    of observed response values, 14,
      17, 20, 21, 49
    of predicted value, 40, 42
    residual, 17, 21
    of sample, 27
    See also Sum of squares.

Wilson, 1, 11, 24

Zelen, 51
Zero
    difference among blocks, 55
    estimate, 34
    mean, 12
    slopes, 32